ACCLAIM FOR SUPERHUMAN

"If we as coaches expect our clients to adapt and learn, then we need to role model doing so. This delightful book gives confidence to the technophobe coach and a wealth of practical tips for the more technology savvy."

—Professor David Clutterbuck
Special Ambassador for the EMCC

"The coaching revolution has started. This book provides you with the insights and knowledge about tools, platforms and apps to be on the right side of the barricades, best able to serve your clients by leveraging technology transforming you into a super-human coach."

—Jonathan Passmore, SVP at CoachHub,
Professor of Coaching & Behavioural Change
at Henley Business School

"The coaching world needs more people like Sam Isaacson! He really gets coaching and he really gets technology. If you're a coach, make sure you read this book."

—Alex Pascal PhD, Founder &
CEO of Coaching.com

"Sam Isaacson cooks up a buffet of coaching technology tools in an easily digestible way. The bite-sized morsels give the reader an enticing taste for cutting edge, emergent technology. This book is for the curious coach who is looking to better understand the future that is happening now or to explore new tools they can use to augment their coaching. Worth adding to your menu of tools!"

—Alicia Hullinger PhD, Executive Director/VP of ICF Thought Leadership Institute

"This is a great collection of technology approaches and digital coaching tools. All coaches should be aware of these and start playing around with them, in order to enhance their coaching practice and be prepared for what's to come in the near future."

—Rebecca Rutschmann, Co-founder & CPO of evoach, host of The Future of Coaching podcast

"Sam Isaacson's latest book explores the possibilities of what can happen when we truly embrace technology alongside our human potential. Reading this book gives you the opportunity to imagine how your coaching practice could evolve beyond time and space, and be ready for tomorrow's world!"

—Lucy Daykin, Head of Coaching at Grant Thornton International

For the courageous and curious

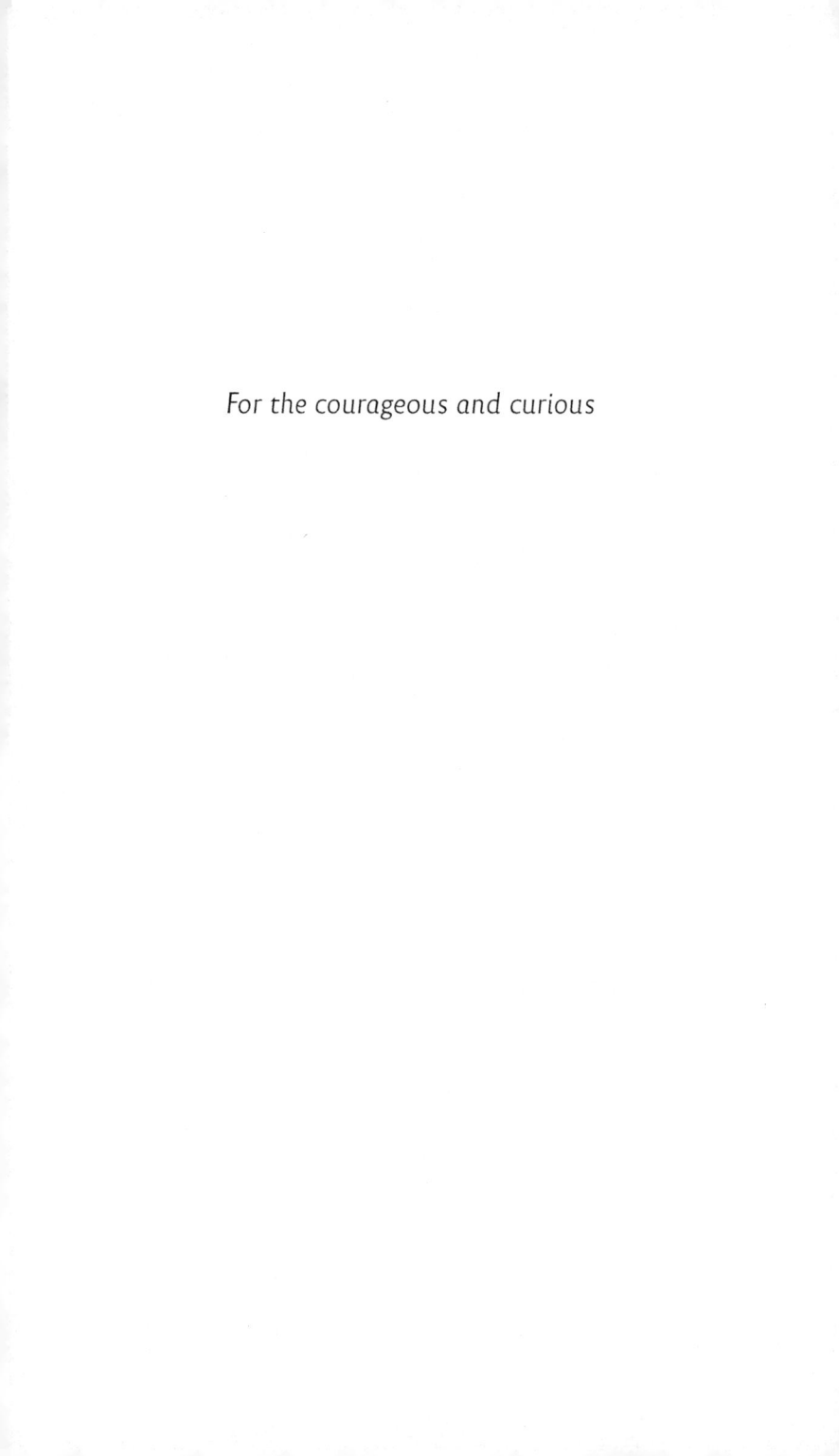

From the author of
How to Thrive as a Coach in a Digital World

SAM ISAACSON

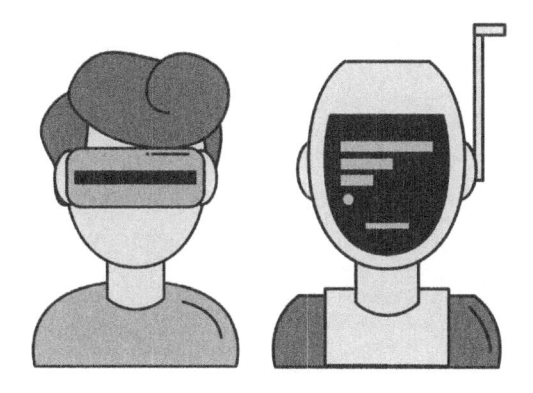

Superhuman Coaching

Ten technologies that expand coaching beyond what's humanly possible

HANWELL
Publishing

Published by Hanwell Publishing in 2022.

Copyright © 2022 Sam Isaacson

All rights reserved. No part of this book may be reproduced or used in any manner without the prior written permission of the copyright owner, except for the use of brief quotations in a book review.

Chapter illustrations by Miranda Reed.
Other images used with permission.

ISBN: 9798836895358

TABLE OF CONTENTS

Acknowledgements ix

Introduction 1

Section 1 Why to go

1 Checking in 6

2 How technology makes us superhuman 17

Section 2 Preparing to launch

3 Screen sharing 35

4 Digital whiteboards 53

5 Digital picture cards 65

6 AI-generated artwork 87

7 Creative writing 99

8 Technology for multisensory coaching 111

9 Constellations 123

10 3D environments 133

11 Exercises in virtual reality 147

12 Virtual reality for meetings 161

Section 3   Setting off

13 The ethics of coachtech 172

14 Defining coachtech 179

ACKNOWLEDGEMENTS

This book has benefited from input from too many people to name individually, so I'd like to begin by thanking everyone that I've had a conversation with, or message from, concerning coaching with technology. Your encouragement and support make such a positive difference, and this book wouldn't exist without you.

A special thanks to the people who have been involved in the process of pushing this through to publication. Faye Kilgour, for the valuable gifts of your time, attention, and advice. All those who have provided permission for screenshots throughout; the descriptions really come alive thanks to you. Those special people who read the book in advance, for your encouragement and wise counsel.

Miranda Reed: The pictures are wonderful. Thank you for your skill and reliability.

Finally, for the most special people in my life: My family. Every day is better because of you.

INTRODUCTION

Over the last couple of years I've had the true privilege of talking to a wide range of coaches from across the planet about coaching with technology. A huge number of those conversations have been intellectually stimulating, dialogues that grapple with the enormity of what the future might hold. Genuinely interesting, mind-stretching, entertaining, challenging...but, if we're honest, without much practical application. They've lacked the tactical, action-focussed impetus that pushes us to do something practical as a result. Thinking about the future is a helpful exercise, and maybe we don't do it properly often enough, but as an outcome-focused coach it feels natural to want to reach something more tangible.

In contrast, the conversations that felt most immediately helpful were those that highlighted one or two technology products that we could start to experiment with later on that day.

This book is designed with that sort of conversation in mind.

It's meant to be practical, walking through a metaphorical gallery of a selection of technology products that will enhance our coaching practice. Perhaps you'll want to follow the arrows from one room to the next, taking in the logical progression as much as the contents of each chapter. Or perhaps you'll dip into selected chapters as your coaching practice continues to evolve.

My hope is that you'll encounter technology in this book you haven't come across before. By the end of the book, you should find yourself feeling intrigued about something new, better equipped to do your own research, and comfortable to find whichever products are most relevant to you, putting them into action as quickly as possible.

A quick note about the book's structure. I wonder if you'd join me in imagining the prospect of an exciting voyage into unknown territory. Perhaps consider the Vikings' first, courageous explorations across the dangerous ocean and into the unknowable West. The first question that needs answering is: Why? What justifies going on this adventure in the first place? We'll therefore begin in Section 1 by laying the groundwork, briefly discussing our natural attitudes towards technology, and exploring why, at a principles level, we ought to engage with it at all.

Section 2 then moves us into a state of getting prepared for the journey, scouting around to ensure we're stocked up as well as possible for what's to come. It's during this section that we'll take our gallery tour, investigating ten different sorts of technology for us to potentially pack in our travel bag.

We'll end in Section 3 with a forward-looking return to our foundations as professional coaches, reminding us of our priorities, and considering the coachtech landscape as a whole. If that all goes to plan, this book ought to act as a springboard that launches us into our futures as superhuman coaches, powered by technology!

By its nature, this book is going to go out of date very quickly. Technology is being updated and made obsolete all the time, so it's inevitable. And the coachtech scene is continually changing shape at the moment. As a result, despite everything being accurate as I'm writing it, in the "now" that you're reading this it's likely that parts of the book are already wrong. For that reason, please take everything in here, particularly anything product-specific, with a pinch of salt. And if you come across technologies that aren't in here that you think might make an interesting new chapter in a new revision, I'd love to hear from you.

I really hope you find the book enjoyable, interesting, and helpful for your coaching practice.

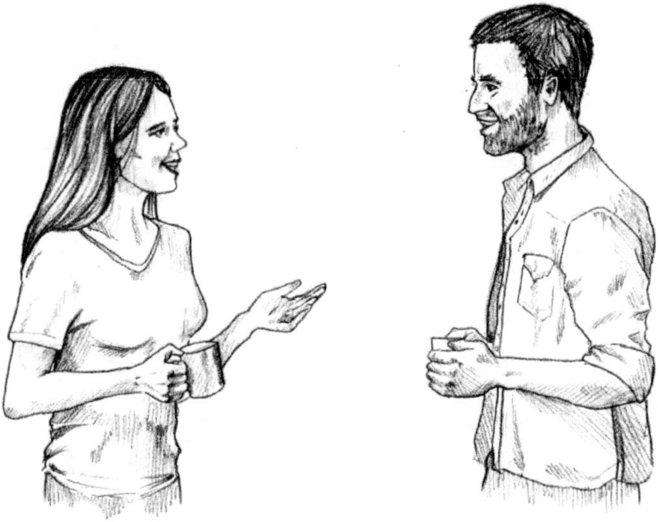

Section 1

Why to go

1

CHECKING IN

Let's begin by pausing. When thinking about technology—or anything, for that matter—we should pay attention to our own natural inclinations. The fact that you're reading this book at all is probably indicative of something or other, but each one of us is unique, and our attitudes towards technology reflect that uniqueness. We all approach technology with our own biases, both conscious and unconscious. We lump certain technologies together, judging the positives and negatives of products and businesses based on isolated data points that may only be connected in our minds. We take news stories and personal experiences and extrapolate out from them, creating almost entirely fictional worldviews that we hold as if they were true. All of this affects our ability to engage with technologies and support others in getting value from them. Increasing our awareness of that can only help.

With that in mind, consider this simple 2x2 matrix (Figure 1.1). We're coaches, we love them, don't we? It offers a simple perspective on the various tendencies we have when approaching new technology.

The X axis captures how much we know about technology. Some of us approach technology feeling like we know almost nothing, confused about how Google seems to know so much about everything. Others of us are highly knowledgeable and experienced in the area, confused about how people don't seem to understand what a VPN is. How about you? If you were pushed, would you say you know less than average about technology, or more than average?

Cutting across that spectrum, the Y axis captures how much we like technology by default. Some people have no problem at all being defined as Luddites, and would rather there be as little technology as possible! For this group, the presentation in the media of the 1950s as a Golden Age might feel like it isn't far enough back into history; a simpler existence characterised by a mediæval village feels a lot more attractive. And yet there are others who seem to want to live in a science fiction dystopia. For this group, a gadget's worth is at least partly defined by whether or not it existed a year before. Again, which side would be most accurate to describe you?

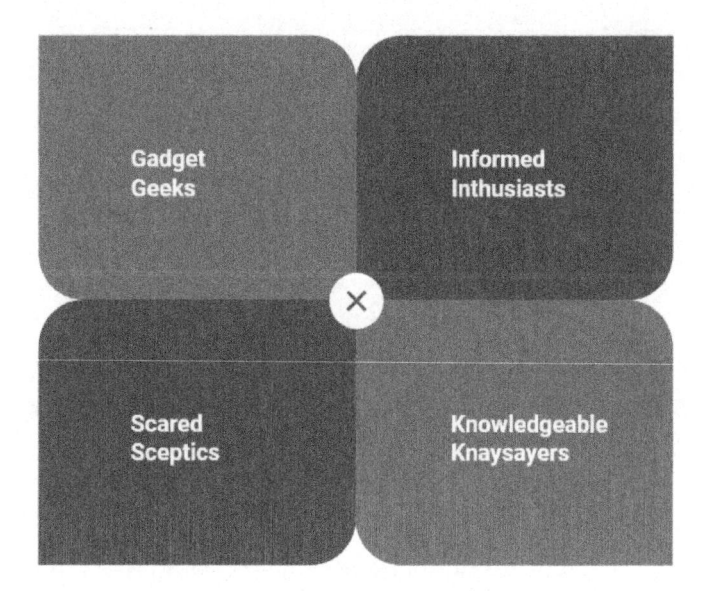

[Matrix figure with four quadrants: Gadget Geeks (top-left), Informed Inthusiasts (top-right), Scared Sceptics (bottom-left), Knowledgeable Knaysayers (bottom-right)]

Figure 1.1 Coachtech attitudes matrix

The value of something like this comes when the axes intersect. Let's spend a moment contemplating each quadrant, to increase our awareness of our own tendencies, as well as those of others.

The bottom-left corner describes those people who don't know very much about technology and, perhaps as a result of this, the topic feels intimidating. The idea that technology is continually changing and increasingly creeping into our consciousness feels to this group like a cause for concern. This sort of person I'll describe here as a **Scared Sceptic**. A judgemental title without doubt, but at least it's alliterative.

A second group may be equally as concerned

about technology's development, but it would be inaccurate to say ·they're simply scared of the unknown. In contrast, their understanding of the field provides more than enough of a reason to not like it. These people understand precisely how security flaws can take shape and be taken advantage of, know that datasets are inherently biased and the reasons that's unavoidable, have heard the stories and rumours emerging from technology companies both big and small, and are profoundly uncomfortable with it all. I'll apologise before saying that I'll call these **Knowledgeable Knaysayers**. If you say it out loud I'm sure you'll agree it has a nice ring to it, despite the clear judgementalism and the embarrassing misuse of the English language.

We've started with those who have a dislike for technology, and I don't need to point out that there are plenty of people who understand technology and are far from sceptical about it. It's probably fair to say that the majority of people who have a real grasp of technology happen to be really enthusiastic about most of it. You've met this sort of person—maybe you are this sort of person. They tend to get excited about the details about technology, and discovering the emergence of a new acronym brings them as much joy as they get from laying their hands on a product that's only just hit the market. These are the ones who can tell you the processing speed of their own devices, and probably yours, and all of the others in general use. And we'll stick with our terrible spelling by calling this group the **Informed Inthusiasts**. Again: sorry.

The final group are just as passionate about technology, but care much less about what's happening behind the scenes. They like the fact that they can switch on lights by speaking to their voice assistant, and that's enough for them. Precisely how their voice is interpreted through semantic triples and turned into electrical signals that cause that to happen isn't interesting enough. This group probably wouldn't mind being called **Gadget Geeks**.

Having read all of that, which group do you find yourself in? If you're not sure (or if you just like self-assessment questionnaires, and who doesn't?), why not complete the short questionnaire at the end of this chapter?

Wherever you are in the grid, an encouragement to all of us ought to be to *continually move towards its right-hand side*. Improving our understanding of how technology works is a good thing for us to do, for a couple of reasons. Firstly, it will help us to make good decisions around which technology to use, and when to use it. The better we understand technology, the more we'll understand its capabilities (and/or capability gaps), and the consequences of using it. We'll also be better qualified to come up with technology solutions that fit our needs. We might even be able to improvise with the technology currently available to us, helping us to establish ourselves as even more brilliantly unique, and most likely adding benefit to our coachees in the process.

Another encouragement would be to *continually move towards the midpoint of the Y axis*. Regardless of how we feel, technology is not objectively good or bad. It's a tool, nothing less and nothing more, and it's neutral in and of itself. We all know that some people have been made extremists through social media, and that's really bad news. At the same time, others have reconnected with old friends and even met the love of their life. Social media is neither good nor bad, it's just a thing. The more we can think about technology from a position of non-judgementalism, the better.

So enjoy the questionnaire, and bear in mind your potential preferences in that matrix as you're reading the rest of the book.

Technology attitude questionnaire

Answer A, B, C, or D for each of the following questions and keep track of your answers.

1. How do you approach email?
   A I have switched my notifications off and much prefer phone calls.
   B I use templates to be as efficient as possible.
   C I'm constantly annoyed by the ping of new emails.
   D I'm constantly checking to see what else I've received.

2. What do you mostly use your mobile phone for?
   A Phone calls and text messages.
   B Communications and banking.
   C I like to leave my phone off unless I need to use it.
   D Entertainment and multitasking.

3. What sort of apps do you download most often?
   A Only the required ones.
   B Anything that looks interesting and with a transparent developer.
   C I'm not sure where to find new apps.
   D Anything with "beta" in the title.

4 How do you feel about laptops?
   A They're a necessary evil.
   B They're a portable, powerful productivity tool.
   C Everything about them is too small.
   D They'd be better if I didn't have to restart them.

5 How would you describe your attitude to artificial intelligence?
   A Not good enough yet and used too widely.
   B A force for efficiency and personalisation.
   C Risky and should be banned.
   D The source of all that's cool in the modern world.

6 What do you most often use internet searches for?
   A The weather and sports scores.
   B Instructional videos and nostalgia.
   C Finding my email and social media.
   D Everything.

7 How much do you use social media?
   A Once a week.
   B Once a day.
   C Only when it pings me.
   D Every spare moment.

8 How would you feel about giving up technology for an extended period of time?
   A Sign me up right now!
   B I'd need to set up some controls for longer than a couple of days.
   C I wish everyone were already fasting technology.
   D Too hard, I couldn't do it.

9 How much do you personally find more possible thanks to technology nowadays in comparison to twenty years ago?
   A Grocery shopping and banking have become more efficient.
   B There's very little I do that doesn't include technology.
   C Almost nothing has changed, although people do smile less.
   D I genuinely don't understand how anyone managed.

10 What impact do you feel technology has on your daily life?
   A I try to keep it as limited as possible.
   B I incorporate technology into everything.
   C Every interaction with technology stresses me out but I can't avoid it.
   D My smartphone is the first thing I wake up to and the last thing I see at night.

CHECKING IN

Now, consult the following with your answers:

- **Mostly As**: You could be a Knowledgeable Knaysayer. You know that technology is a part of the modern world, and try to limit your use of it. You might benefit from thinking more broadly about what value technology could add to your life and your coaching practice.
- **Mostly Bs**: You could be an Informed Inthusiast. You understand technology, and try to make the most of it. You might overwhelm people with how much you know and how intuitive you find it, so might want to think about what impact your use of technology might have on your coachees.
- **Mostly Cs**: You could be a Scared Sceptic. You don't like technology and find that it encroaches on your life in frustrating ways. You would do well to take some time out to really get to know the technology you have to use most often, and discover that your dislike might come from a lack of familiarity more than anything else.
- **Mostly Ds**: You could be a Gadget Geek. You love new technology and can't wait to try out the next big thing. At times you might be exposing yourself and your coachees to unreasonable risks, so should get to know some of the concepts that lie behind the technology you use most often.

Before we dive into the meat of Section 2, let's use the next chapter to really dig into why technology is worth spending our time thinking about.

2

HOW TECHNOLOGY MAKES US SUPERHUMAN

Coaching, at its heart, is fundamentally human. To add technology into a coaching conversation could be seen as a distraction, reducing its impact. We should always be mindful of this being the case, so it's important to directly address the issue of why we might ever want to use technology in a coaching context.

One valid reason might be that we have no choice in the matter. If a coachee with a clear need will have no access to coaching unless technology is involved, its justification is self-evident. So, when a big organisation decides to exclusively use one particular digital coaching provider to offer coaching to its employees, the choice around that coaching is a binary one: Deliver through the technology, or don't deliver any coaching.

There are other reasons as well. To understand that, it's worth asking why we might want to use technology in *any* context. And to answer that question, it's worth taking a surprising turn.

Every few years, an unexpected fact rears its head again, reminding us that reality is more complex than our actions betray we believe. One of those facts is that cows have four stomachs. It seems odd even when you know it's true. Regurgitating grass in order to chew it forever seems strange, doesn't it? Why don't they have just one stomach, like us?

Disappointingly, it turns out that cows actually *do* only have one stomach like us, but unlike us have a stomach containing four distinct compartments. Less disappointingly, and much more curiously, it turns out that humans, in a way, don't actually only have one stomach. Or, more accurately, we use technology as a quasi second stomach. Humans use technology to do the work we'd otherwise need a more complex digestive system for. Perhaps it's the earliest example of technology. Humans have many unique characteristics that distinguish us from the more than human world, but this one is probably the most fundamental: We can manipulate fire.

The impact of technology

Fire does many things. It keeps us warm, so we can survive in some of the harshest environments we'd simply die in otherwise. It scares predators, protecting us from attack. It provides a focal point to allow communities to be built. And it can be used to prepare food, which turns out to be an extraordinary building block for everything we've achieved as a species.[1] We can cook meat, killing off the harmful bacteria that have led many carnivores to need an accelerated digestive system. We can cook vegetables, breaking down the tougher pieces. Our control of fire allows us to eat pretty much anything that's within reach, giving us the energy we need, even when times are hard. And cooked food provides much more energy than raw food does, freeing up our time and our bodies' development to concentrate on higher impact areas.

So fire acts as a first stomach for us, one that sits outside of our bodies. That gives us a biological advantage. We have more time to think than animals that don't cook, our bodies can focus energy on developing our prefrontal cortex rather than digesting food, and we can eat pretty much at will, making us extraordinarily adaptable.

The foundational impacts of technology don't stop there. The other big technological breakthrough that defines our species is the wheel, which does something similar to fire. The technology extends our bodily capabilities outside of ourselves, essentially giving us superpowered legs. A human with access to the wheel is able to travel much

[1] For more information, see Wrangham, R. (2010). *Catching Fire: How Cooking Made Us Human*. Profile Books.

faster, and for a far longer period of time. This naturally gives a competitive advantage, and has contributed towards humans becoming the dominant species in every environment that we've chosen to enter.

Imagine living in a community that hasn't developed the wheel. When faced with a natural threat like a flood, or a human threat like an attack from a neighbouring tribe, your ability to escape is going to be restricted. You can only travel a certain distance, you can only travel at a certain speed, and you can only carry a certain amount. But the village a mile up the road that has the wheel can move more quickly, for longer, and can carry more equipment and supplies. They can even transport people who would be entirely incapable of moving further than a short distance otherwise.

In your eyes, you'd have no option other than to consider the people in that village superhuman. With their enhanced, augmented capabilities there's something about them that makes them perhaps inspiring, probably intimidating, maybe even terrifying. They deal with reality in a way that you can't, and the only real difference is the technology that they have access to.

Psychotechnologies

Perhaps the wheel isn't the best example, because it's so visible. The real power of technology to turn us into superhumans comes when we move into the realm of *psychotechnologies*. Technologies such as the manipulation of fire and the wheel are concerned with extending the abilities of our body outside of ourselves. Psychotechnologies are concerned with extending the abilities of our mind.

What if you were a part of a different village, which has the wheel, but in this case hasn't developed writing? That neighbouring village, this time capable of writing, would be incomprehensible. Through some apparent magic, they have the ability to solve complex problems, and remember things collectively, even across generations. More than that, they seem capable of thinking through extremely complex problems, rapidly accelerating their abilities across a whole range of disciplines.

And this experience is one many are experiencing in the present world. Some people have access to technologies that seem to make them superhuman, and those technologies are developing faster than anyone can keep up with. A select group of people seems to be capable of achieving the impossible across multiple specialist areas, leaving the rest of humanity behind. The nature of exponential growth is that it doesn't matter which point of the accelerating corner you're sitting at. If you're primarily looking into the past, it will always appear as if everything's about to explode out of all control. The superhumans with access to the technology are already one step ahead, and not moving is only going to increase that distance.

The answer to the question of why we might want to use technology therefore turns out to be simple: Technology, at least in theory, can make us better coaches. The opportunities it affords us are very great. If we can get the hang of technology, we will become superhuman coaches, capable of achieving the seemingly impossible for those we're working with. Coaches that use technology well in their practice will often be experienced as the most creative, dynamic, and insightful coaches, because the technology is making them better. Their coaching is superhuman coaching, because the technology is adding something to it.

To understand this in practice, it might help to think about the ways technology helps us through three primary purposes: Technology expands our capacity, enhances our competence, and extends our capability.

Technology expands our capacity

Some technology is straightforward enough to grasp. It does something we're already able to do, taking it off our plate and opening up greater possibilities. Let's take the example of a robot vacuum cleaner, which quite clearly performs a task most of us are already able to do. If a robot vacuum cleaner is introduced into our lives, the time we previously took vacuuming can be used for whatever we want, if we're wise enough about it.

We might choose to use that time to achieve something different, or we might consciously use the time to do the same thing, but better. The introduction of the handheld vacuum cleaner demonstrated this starkly. In spite of its luxurious promises to bring a new era of leisure to those that spent all their time cleaning, the vacuum cleaner didn't appear to save anyone any time after all. Instead, the expectations of how tidy a home ought to be were increased. As we gain access to new technology that automates tasks we would otherwise be performing ourselves, we can consciously choose to do something better, or unconsciously be pulled into doing something different. Of course, we could choose to use the time it frees up to simply relax, but the experience of most people nowadays is that rest doesn't come naturally. We tend to fill downtime with a different sort of busyness, pursuing leisure through entertainment technologies rather than pursuing rest through relaxation.

When this sort of technology takes a task or two off our plate we get the extra time, allowing us to focus our attention elsewhere. In the world of coaching, that might look like coaching software such as Delenta[2] or Coaching.com,[3] which automate coaching management processes that would

[2] https://www.delenta.com/

[3] https://www.coaching.com/

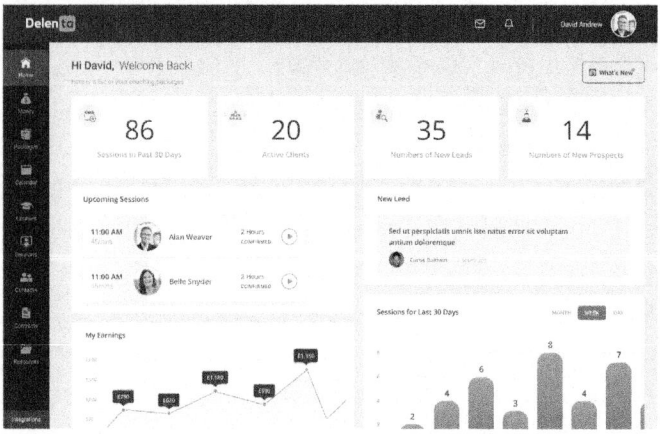

Figure 2.1 A dashboard from the Delenta coaching platform

otherwise take up significant amounts of time. Whether this newfound capacity will be used for business development, personal development, or scrolling endlessly through Instagram, will be down to the individual coach.

Technology enhances our competence

The second contribution technology makes is to improve and augment the things we're already able to do. The technology of binoculars, for example, improves our ability to see, and transportation technology increases our speed and journey length.

In a coaching context, this might look like a technology that allows us to speed up or improve something we do in a coaching session. We'll look at plenty of these in the coming pages, because these

HOW TECHNOLOGY MAKES US SUPERHUMAN 25

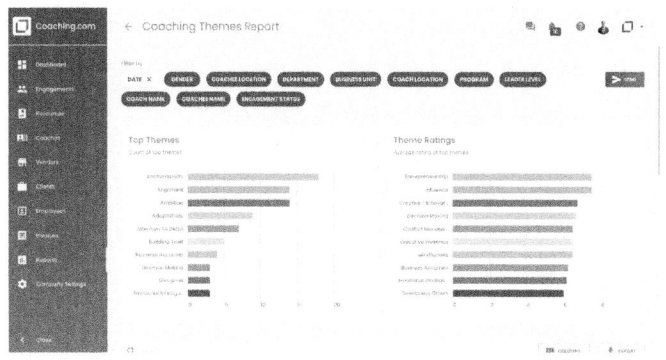

Figure 2.2 A report from Coaching.com

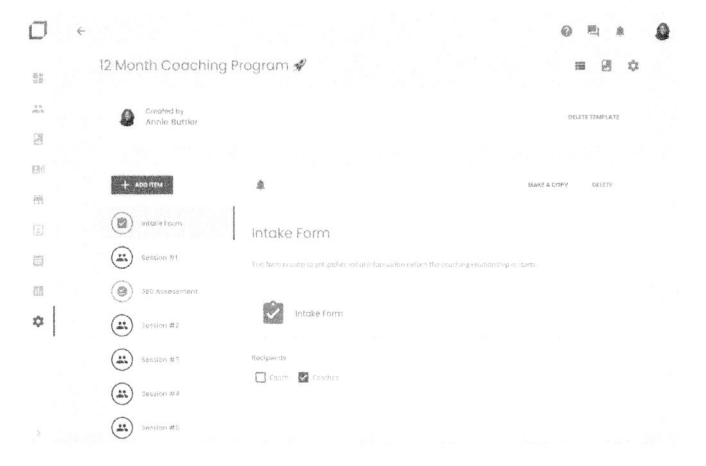

Figure 2.3 A screen from Coaching.com showing different elements of a coaching engagement

technologies are by far the easiest to introduce into our lives. The technology of contactless payments has been adopted quickly in comparison to other technologies because it sped up something that was already happening, and required less effort in the process. As a simple coaching example, imagine a coach deciding in a session to recommend a good video for the coachee to watch. During an in-person coaching session, the coach might describe the video, and promise to find it and email it across later. They make a note, and one would hope they'll remember to send the link over when they're next in front of their email. Using video conferencing allows the coach to almost instantly copy-paste the video link into the chat.

This is the most common sort of technology we should be thinking about as coaches. We're already effective enough at delivering coaching, so we're starting from a good position. What technology can offer us to bring that superhuman element is where it can make it even better for all the stakeholders involved.

Technology extends our capability

The final thing technology does is enable us to do entirely new things. Technology enabled ancient civilisations to build ships, turning rivers and oceans from barriers into transport highways. It opened up new possibilities of written communication through the printing press, rapidly accelerating education around the world. It allowed Nathan Evans to sing in harmony with his own voice multiple times, propelling him into the public eye with his version of the sea shanty *The Wellerman*.[4] Some of the things

[4] https://www.tiktok.com/@nathanevanss/video/6910995345421962498

HOW TECHNOLOGY MAKES US SUPERHUMAN 27

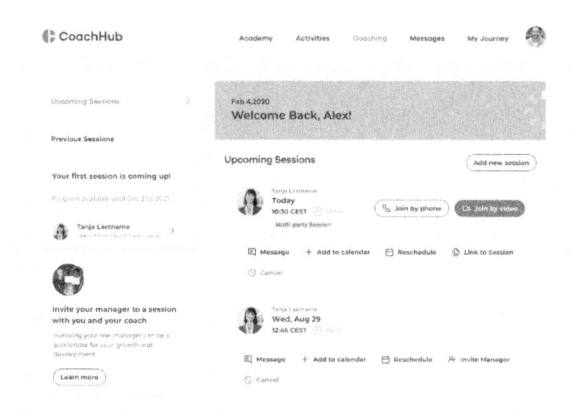

Figure 2.4 A screen from CoachHub showing upcoming sessions

Figure 2.5 A screen from CoachHub showing a dashboard

we do every day now would be impossible without technology.

Perhaps the best coaching-specific example of this would be digital coaching providers like

CoachHub,[5] which provide global access to an enormous pool of coaches at extremely competitive rates. Organisations get to introduce coaching at massive scales that were previously impossible, and coaches get to replace a lot of their business development time with coaching delivery.

Digital coaching providers aren't the only technology that's disrupting the coaching profession. Increasing use of technology from every angle is forcing us all to rethink how we're approaching everything. While the coaching profession isn't as old as many others, it's fair to say that there are several aspects of it that still operate the same way they always have. When a technology provider emerges that changes organisational or consumer behaviour, coaches will have to adapt. Maybe that will be to do with changes in communications technology, or artificial intelligence, or the metaverse, or blockchain technology, or neural interfaces, or something else. The future is unknown, and therefore difficult to plan for; suffice it to say that this aspect of technology is the most disruptive of the three.

Technology and tradeoffs

The Dinka people of South Sudan are a great example of the superhuman effect that technology offers. Traditionally, they capture the life stories of each individual in the group through an extremely

https://www.coachhub.com/

long, personal song composed by a particularly gifted person called a "Ping"—literally "The Hearer"— who will sing this important song once for you, and only once. In the past, this was a concern: How can I remember my own song? But the tape recorder came along and changed all of that. A member of the Dinka recording the song being sung will have a perfect record for all time![6]

But the introduction of this technology ought to make anyone question: Doesn't the introduction of such a disruptive technology, however positive the effects, also have a downside? In the case of the Dinka, the Ping role has been downgraded in importance; you no longer need to take one along with you to help you remember your song. And perhaps that's a justified tradeoff when considering the bigger picture; on balance, the entire people group is better off.

Perhaps not.

Whenever we introduce technology into a coaching relationship, it's likely to come with tradeoffs. In some cases, the transaction is transparent and has a clear business case, while in others the negative side of the balance may be more significant, and we should pay attention to it. I wrote about this a lot more in my previous book, *How to Thrive as a Coach in a Digital World*, so I won't repeat myself. For now, I'll simply point out that this book is not an evangelistic tract for technology. The

[6]Visit https://youtu.be/sQEETH-CzK8?t=479 to hear the full story in a lot more detail.

chapters in the next section are intended as a helpful selection to increase our awareness, and are not specifically recommendations. Specifically, they're not all universal recommendations. If anyone ends up using everything written about in here, they're probably using far too much technology in their coaching!

Ten to get started with

With this all in mind, the next section will look at ten sorts of technology that we might want to consider to make our coaching superhuman. As we go through them together, let's bear in mind that these are intended to be applicable across the coaching profession broadly, and therefore won't be a good fit for every coach everywhere. This is not intended to be a "top ten" that every coach should use. They're simply ideas to get the ball rolling, and if our readings and reflections lead us to start using something entirely different, that's wonderful.

All ten chapters should have enough practical information in them to enable even the most inexperienced of us to start using the technology almost straight away. Very little in the coming pages is speculation around the future of coachtech, the technology in each chapter already exists. With every tool active and available, let's commit together to remain curious, and experiment with anything that piques our interest.

With one very obvious exception (you'll know it when you see it), no specialist equipment or high-end internet connection is required for any of these, and I've tried to be as transparent as possible around pricing. These enhanced experiences should be as accessible as possible.

The section contains ten chapters in loose pairs, looking at technologies across five semi-categories:

- Technology for collaboration: screen sharing and digital whiteboards
- Technology that introduces new visual stimuli to the session: digital picture card decks and AI-generated artwork
- Technology that induces creative thinking using other senses: creative writing tools and soundscapes
- Technology that catalyses systemic coaching: constellations-related products and virtual worlds
- Technology using virtual reality (VR): exercises activated in VR for in-person coaching, and VR as a way to meet remotely

Section 2

Preparing to launch

3

SCREEN SHARING

When going on a journey, we can only start from where we currently are. In the case of coaches, the majority that I speak to would say that the most commonly used piece of technology in their delivery toolkit is some video conferencing service or other. One function that's worth particularly picking out to enhance coaching would be the "screen share" button. A well-timed, elegantly selected moment that breaks across the conversation might do more to spark insights than the most cleverly articulated coaching question. Adding variety to a coaching conversation can activate parts of our coachees' minds that otherwise might remain "offline". The coaching questions a coachee will ask themselves silently when we simply present something will take them to places we couldn't take them using only words. In terms of ways to enhance a coaching conversation and do it with the lightest addition of technology, it's hard to think of much else. Let's think about some practicalities.

Screen sharing is a broad concept. We could share any window we have open or ask a coachee to, illuminating parts of a conversation and generating insight that wouldn't otherwise be present. To keep things simple, for the moment let's just talk about presentation software like Microsoft PowerPoint.

Because PowerPoint is so widely used, it doesn't feel as exciting as other tools we'll look at. Maybe that's for good reason. We've all seen PowerPoint used in ways that make it feel dull. Bland slides full of text to accompany a bland presentation. But the joy of this sort of software is its flexibility, as well as every coachee's familiarity with it, eliminating the "IT onboarding" baggage other tools might come with.

The thing with PowerPoint is that you can put anything you like on a slide and present it precisely as you'd like it. There are countless templates available for download, and even the most complex ideas are easy to add to a slide. A quick internet search for someone else's hard work, copy-pasted into our file, and we've easily avoided the effort required to recreate them (providing we're not breaching copyright, which would be illegal and immoral). With that in mind, let's think about four ways we can use it in practice, and then go on to discuss what a good next step might look like.

Conceptual models

One way to use screen sharing to enhance a coaching conversation is to introduce a frame for discussion. One simple example of this that almost all coaches find themselves grappling with at one time or another would be psychometrics. Some of these are simpler than others, and debates around the scientific validity of specific products will rage for as long as debaters want them to, but even the biggest cynic would have to concede that they have undeniable advantages.

The biggest of these is that they provide a common language for self reflection and increased awareness. For example, the overly simplistic four colours of the Insights Discovery model[7] is the key behind its success. Despite every certified facilitator insisting on using the phrase "has a preference for Sunshine Yellow energy", everyone who encounters it needs no prompting before they start describing themselves and other people as simply being red or blue. Even using it clumsily, the insights and emotional intelligence unlocked by that are clear.

The tool in question could be mumbo jumbo. Indeed, there are plenty out there that essentially are —we're all likely to have stumbled across "personality tests" that claim to reveal something about us based on our name or something equally arbitrary providing we expose ourselves to adverts. We should hold evidence-based, truly scientific

[7] https://www.insights.com/products/insights-discovery/

models in high regard, while still recognising that part of their helpfulness purely comes from seeing these things through the lens of self awareness. Even just looking at a simplified overview of a psychometric might be enough to dramatically increase a coachee's self awareness, perhaps far more than a coach could achieve through any length of intelligent questioning.

There's no need to point out that this is broader than psychometrics. Many leadership models are carefully designed to be presented on one page. We should make the most of that, and present them to our coachees where they would find this most helpful. This is all exactly the sort of thing coaches have been doing forever with coachees, and it doesn't mean telling a coachee how they ought to act. We need to be careful to not turn a coaching session into a 1:1 training webinar. Instead, by non-judgmentally sharing a pre-existing model, preferably based on solid research, we provide our coachees with a new frame of reference for their thinking and being.

An alternative model to share might be a coaching model, straight out of the textbook. A simple slide with the GROW elements (goal, reality, options, way forward) presented nicely on a slide, can give coachees a quick overview of where the conversation could go, with two clear advantages.

Firstly, we suddenly find ourselves more tied down to remaining true to a model in its purest form. That isn't always desirable—it's often nice to have the flexibility to chop and change as we go—but at times, particularly when we're less experienced with a model, sticking to its principles as it was designed offers benefits we end up missing out on if we lose heart halfway through.

Secondly, the coachee gets to see where the conversation is heading from the get-go, meaning they already start answering future questions in their head before they encounter them. Again, that might not always be desirable—with something like Nancy Kline's Thinking Environment,[8] the space given to the opening questions is intentionally so great that not getting any further is a common, and helpful, experience.

With all of these, it's important to note that they're not there as a silver bullet to be used in every coaching session. Using them with intelligence and clear intuition will make them much more likely to be effective. What we're doing here is no different from what we might want to do if we were coaching in person. It wouldn't be uncommon for a coach to have printed something out as part of their preparation, and in other cases we might find ourselves scribbling a quick 2x2 matrix or Venn diagram onto a sheet of paper. The only difference is the medium.

---

[8] See Kline, N. (2015). *More Time to Think: The Power of Independent Thinking*. Cassell

Words

The visual diagrams described above are one thing, but at other times a coachee might need something a bit different. An informational or inspirational quote can be helpful to bring in an alternative viewpoint in a non-judgmental way. At times, a full paragraph of text or a short book summary could add something to a coaching session.

All of this needs preparation—it isn't a good use of time to search for a helpful page in a relevant book live in a coaching session. We'll come onto the practicalities of that in a moment, in view of the importance of positioning ourselves well to do something like this for our coachees. A good exercise for now would be to put some thought towards the key topics it would be helpful to have something on hand for, to equip ourselves appropriately before the time comes that we need to use them.

Pictures

We've talked about introducing insightful content into coaching sessions as a way of sparking new thinking, and that can be exciting; which coach doesn't love a good one page summary of a leadership model? Sometimes, though, the coachee doesn't need more content. Quite the opposite, particularly with those coachees whose minds have

Figure 3.1 An image for exploration.

already been whirring with whatever their current issue is. I'm a coachee myself, and my coach has asked me more than once if the explanation I'm giving in response to a question is for my benefit, as I explore some new line of thinking, or hers, as I explain to her the same rehearsed narrative I've been playing through my mind for the past several days. Sometimes, when we're coaching people, the coachee has asked themselves the same questions on repeat since the idea first entered their mind, and the questions we're asking are unlikely to unlock anything truly new.

But this is a space that coaching operates extremely well in. Sometimes highly cognitive, linear processing doesn't work. The surprise question we hold in our back pocket that makes connections between two unconnected things works wonders for people whose minds are well-trained in traditional problem-solving. It disrupts them in a good way, catalysing something new. When a coachee has spent several weeks going back and forth on how to deal with a new employee whose character they find difficult, we need to support them in breaking through that stuck thinking. Asking them which stick person in the image (Figure 3.1) represents both them and their new colleague at one level means nothing, and yet at the same time might bring a level of clarity that previously was impossible to access.

The few minutes it took me to create that could be extended by a few more to drop it onto a slide, ready to share in a coaching session. And we don't even have to create it ourselves. Websites like Unsplash[9] provide access to thousands of beautiful images, and art galleries have moved many collections online. In fact, one thing the internet has no shortage of is images to communicate pretty much any situation we can imagine, and some we can't! The photo I stumbled across a few years ago of a pair of donkeys in a paddling pool wearing sunhats in front of a car on fire won't leave me, and would be wonderful as a catalyst for creative thinking in some coaching sessions. More on all of this in chapters 5 and 6.

Interactivity

The stick person tool above works perfectly well as a static image, and can sometimes unlock all sorts of

[9] https://www.unsplash.com/

SCREEN SHARING 43

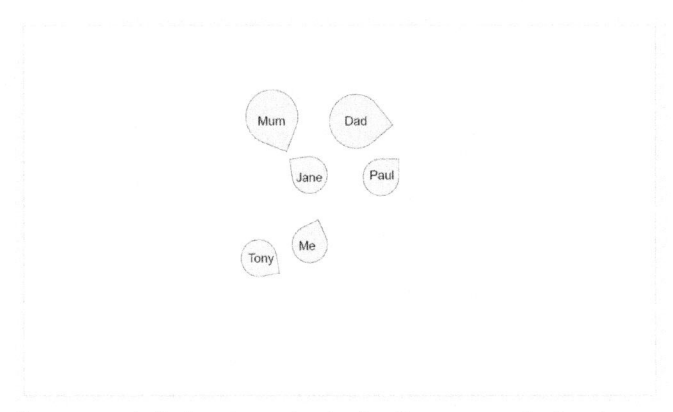

Figure 3.2 A fictional coachee's family system, depicted on a slide

new thinking thanks to that simple prompt. How could we take that one step further?

What would happen if, instead of sharing the entire image with a coachee, the coach instead shared just the background, and gave the coachee full control over where they would put themselves, their size, and their stance? Many coaches are familiar with the concept of systemic constellations, in which a coachee places physical objects in a particular configuration to represent relationships between people they're connected to. We'll talk about this in much more detail in chapters 9 and 10. It's relatively straightforward to recreate some elements of that experience in a remote coaching session, simply by sharing the screen and allowing the coachee to place shapes on a blank slide.

You can see an example of what it might look like in Figure 3.2. In this instance, a fictional coachee, let's call her Sarah, identifies herself as "Me",

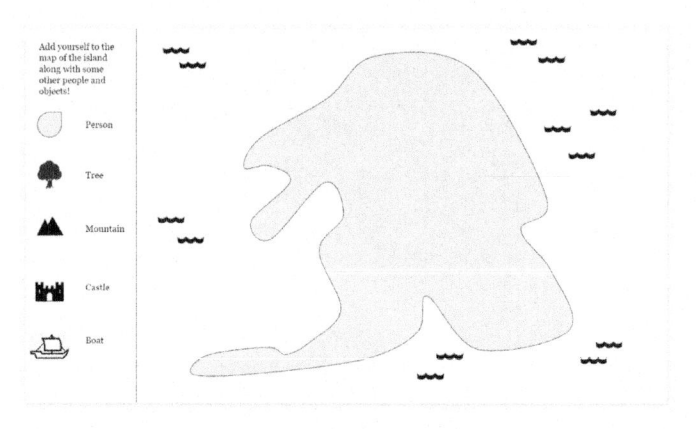

Figure 3.3 A template for use in a coaching session

putting herself towards the middle of the slide. With control of the screen, she places members of her family system elsewhere. Perhaps her coach will invite her to consider what things look like from different family members' perspectives, or experiment with moving the shapes around to a desired future state.

Having said that, let's just pause for a moment on the idea of a blank slide, because that won't be the most helpful starting spot for every coachee. While it's beautifully non-directive, sometimes a template with limited options can be helpful to catalyse some action. Asking a coachee to "add a shape" can induce analysis paralysis, while asking them instead, "Is your boss better represented by this triangle or this circle?" might more quickly generate insights. And nothing's stopping the coachee replying something like: "Actually, I think they're more like a square, can I create one of those?"

Similarly, providing a background that gives them more than just a blank page might be helpful. Introducing a couple of landmarks, such as those illustrated in Figure 3.3, that a coachee assigns meaning to—even without explaining them to us—might help them rapidly identify connections between concepts, people, and activities that previously felt too complex to understand.

Ways to do it

We've talked about some ways we can share our screen to enhance a coaching session. Let's think practically now about what we need to do to make that as seamless an experience for both coach and coachee as possible. The simple takeaway from this should be: Prepare it well. If we do that, we'll effortlessly guide our coachees through an experience in a non-directive way that offers them new insights and memorable experiences. Precisely how to prepare will be different for each one of us.

For some, the right way to approach this will be to steadily build one central repository of screen-sharing goodness. One slide deck perhaps, where each slide or sequence of slides includes a model, image, exercise, or something else. There are two big advantages that come with this approach. Firstly, it can be built over time in a natural way. When we stumble across something and think it might be helpful, we know exactly where to put it. Open up the deck, drop it in, and our day can continue. Secondly, less time is required to think in detail to plan a coaching session. If that file's open, we're ready for anything, and can dive into whichever place we want to at a moment's notice.

This "one slide deck to rule them all" approach does have its downsides, however. If it's too big, it can take a long time to find what we're looking for in it, and no coachee wants to watch us scrolling endlessly through slide after slide. This becomes an even bigger problem if we're sharing our screen while we're doing it. Some coachees have a tendency to be distracted when they see a slide we weren't intending to share. Just because someone's seen Maslow's Hierarchy before and wants to tell a story about it doesn't make that a helpful use of the time, although I do like to think that tangents and distractions can often be more telling than the core essence of a coaching conversation. It's worth acknowledging that there is no such thing as going off on a tangent, only an increasing realisation that the complexity of reality means that connections exist.

Secondly, the size of the file and the speed of our network connection will directly affect how quickly our computer can deal with it. A deck containing a hundred slides full of multimedia and transition animations will take a lot of time to load, and will be slow to navigate, while a deck of ten slides of single words will offer a more streamlined experience.

An alternative approach might therefore be to pull together a selection of different files depending on a categorisation logic that seems to make sense. So there might be one slide deck with book summaries, another one with pleasant images, and another containing leadership models. Or they might be gathered by topic—a handful of different ideas that might help with time management in this one, and some thoughts that might support a conversation around executive presence in that one. As with everything else, the strength of this approach is its weakness. The time saved through not flicking through slides is replaced most likely with time wading through a folder structure that probably made sense at the time it was created. And my personal experience of folder structures is that the sense that was used to construct it gets lost to the sands of time faster than I anticipate.

And so a third approach raises its head, with a promise of greater efficiency and personalisation for each coachee, the tradeoff being extra effort on the part of the coach. This would be a hybrid approach, with one central repository as the coach's personal library, along with a unique file for each coachee. Before each coaching session, we can open up our big file and extract the most relevant slides, pasting them into a new file to streamline its use within the session itself. That style will work for some coaches and not for others.

Some of us might feel it too risky, as we might make false assumptions and line up the wrong content, and then feel hamstrung by the restricted choices, making us less effective overall.

Also, video

Thinking more broadly than static images draws us naturally towards moving pictures, beckoning us into the black hole that is video on the internet. Most coaches are fully aware of the wealth of TED talks, visual book summaries, stirring spoken word films and helpful animations accessible out there. Indeed, plenty of us have tried to help our coachees by recommending an inspirational video as homework (a term I think every coach has a love-hate relationship with), hoping and expecting they'll get as much value from it as we did when we watched it for the first time.

But how many coachees make the time to watch that video? And of those who do, how many are truly concentrating on it, making notes, and taking time throughout and/or afterwards to reflect on how they might actively apply whatever was discussed in it? Few, I'd wager. What's the solution?

This one takes some effort, because videos use up a certain amount of time. That's the challenge. It takes time to plan to use them, and it takes time to use them in the time-limited session. A clip of longer than two-three minutes feels like it's eating into valuable coaching time. We therefore ought to set time aside outside of the coaching sessions to

Figure 3.4 The YouTube share popup

watch back those favourite talks and animations, with an eye on selecting the best minute or two from them, and then making a note for future reference.

The slickest way to do this would be to create a custom link for ourselves that starts at the perfect time. On YouTube, this is relatively straightforward. Clicking the Share button under the video opens up a small window with a tickbox at the bottom. Clicking on the tickbox adds some text to the URL, coding in the right number of seconds to skip so that the link will take us to wherever we've reached in the video. Copying that URL and saving it in a bookmarks folder, or cleverly embedding it in a slide deck, means that every time we click on it, we'll skip to the most impactful moment.

A final word of caution

We raised earlier in the chapter the risk of screen sharing turning a coaching session into something it shouldn't be. If this practice is something we adopt and find value in, it would be worth bringing it to supervision to reflect on where the value's lying. It can be a way to inject high-quality content and better thinking into a coaching conversation, and it can also replace high-quality, intense moments of coach-coachee magic with something else.

Screen sharing should be considered low-hanging fruit if we're delivering remote coaching, as it's almost certainly easily accessible. But just because we *can* do something doesn't mean that we *should*.

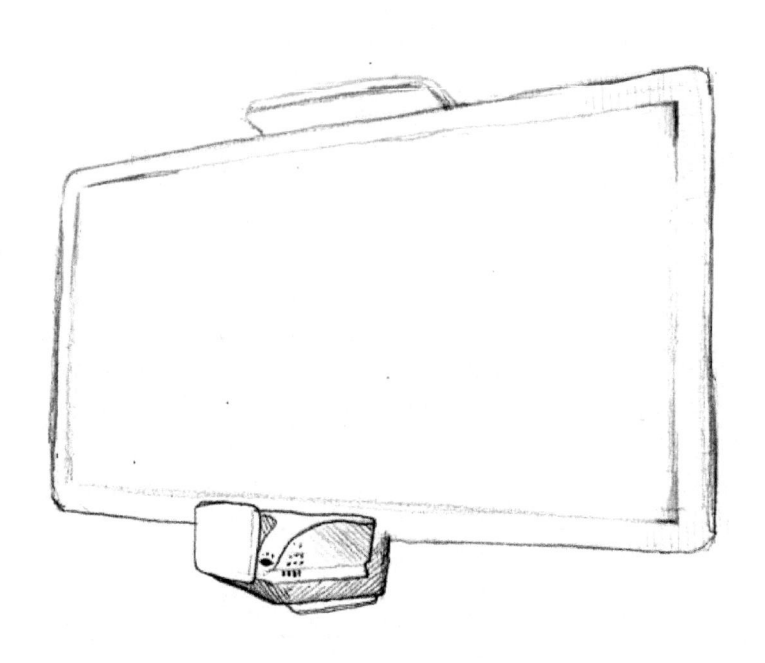

4

DIGITAL WHITEBOARDS

Think back with me to the beginning of 2020, just before the COVID-19 lockdowns first came into effect. One of the biggest hesitations people had about conducting meetings remotely used to be the perceived lack of ability to collaborate. Writing messages in the chat window is nice enough, but it isn't the same as everybody moving sticky notes around on the wall. It isn't surprising, therefore, that one of the technology products that did really well in 2020 was digital whiteboards. Ask a random selection of coaches which technologies they use in their coaching, and, after video conferencing, digital whiteboards will be a common answer.

These tools lend themselves by design to a well-managed, non-directive experience. The spaces they offer can be enormous and extremely flexible, and importantly they allow multiple people to make additions and changes on their own terms.

The most obvious use case for digital whiteboards would be team coaching. Several people connecting to the board are able to make changes separately as individuals, while remaining connected to the whole. The insights coaching could generate for a team based purely on how they interact in that space could be very good.

The most popular standalone whiteboard tools come supercharged with capabilities. The product philosophy behind them reaches far beyond how many coaches will want to use them, and so the possibilities for their use can feel limitless. We'll come back to that at the end of the chapter, and why that's not necessarily a good thing, but before we get there let's explore a handful of applications for digital whiteboards in coaching sessions.

Brainstorms

The simplest application for a digital whiteboard is as a space to collect thoughts and ideas from multiple people simultaneously. Thinking specifically about team coaching for a moment, let's imagine we want to run a session in which each member of the team contributes their own thoughts about what the team's shared purpose is, or ought to be. Using purely a video conferencing tool, the exercise of simply hearing what each team member initially thinks could easily end up lasting more than half an hour. It turns out that video calls cause us to pay more visible attention, most likely leading to so-called "Zoom fatigue", extending the amount of time each person speaks for, and demonstrably reducing the level of creativity.[10]

Compare that with giving the entire team just a few, uninterrupted minutes of capturing their ideas succinctly on sticky notes, away from the video call screen, then giving them a chance to read each other's and adding a mark to those they agree with. Within a quarter of an hour, everyone will have contributed, and we can then lead a discussion around the outputs. Extraordinary efficiency.

It can work in 1:1 settings too. Coach and coachee might want to come up with a list of options together, and the sticky note feature provides a chance to hurl a varied range of ideas up there in a non-hierarchical way, while it feels difficult to contribute ideas verbally without them sounding like suggestions.

Structured exercises

In the previous chapter we looked at the idea of providing a populated slide to give a coachee an insightful experience. The same is true when using a digital whiteboard, and more than that, the possibilities become much greater. At a simple level,

[10]Brucks, M.S., Levav, J. Virtual communication curbs creative idea generation. *Nature 605*, 108–112 (2022).

the size of the map of the island (using the example from the previous chapter) is no longer limited to one slide. Digital whiteboards allow us to zoom in and out so much more, exploring space that by its nature simply doesn't exist when using a slide. This allows for all sorts of exploratory metaphor and storytelling, opening up greater awareness in a coachee of the narratives they tell themselves.

And, in the same way that we discussed in the previous chapter, this freedom can also cause problems of its own. How can a coachee be expected to discover the assumptions they hold through an almost directionless activity, when they might not even realise they hold assumptions? Pre-populated templates are the way forward, creating a toolkit of exercises to dive into with the coachee, depending on what sort of situation they bring.

For example, imagine a coachee saying they're having difficulty in their marriage. We might already have a template prepared that simply has a collection of icons available, alongside a chart showing positivity over time. By asking the coachee to draw a line on the chart, and annotate it only using those icons, they're empowered to discover something new about their relationship experience, supporting them in clarifying a way forward that will work for them and their spouse.

Something digital whiteboards can be really good at is helping to map out systems, however complex. Because the canvas can be manipulated much more than a slide can, and the shapes tend to be fewer clicks away, a coachee's ability to recreate their internal systems landscape is accelerated. Stakeholder mapping exercises and systemic constellations lend themselves particularly well to digital whiteboards.

At the end of the session

Digital whiteboards offer far more choices than we get from a simple screen share, and certainly more than an in-person coaching experience would grant without an equivalent tool. And digital whiteboards offer one more piece of functionality that's critically important.

I led an exercise with a coachee in person recently, where he plotted his career experience and desired future state along a timeline he was imagining. We picked up a handful of items to hand, and he quickly assigned them meaning and gained new insights into his life to date, as well as what he might want to do next.

At the end of the session, I asked him whether he'd like me to take a photo of what he'd created. "No, that's fine," he replied, "I've got what I needed to from the conversation." Maybe that was true, maybe he was trying to be polite, or maybe he didn't realise that he'd want that image in six months' time. Regardless, the only way he could take the experience with him would be through a photograph and his memories.

A digital whiteboard is different. We can export it as an image, or simply share a screenshot of the output, for their reflection at some point in the future. More than that, we could share a link to it, allowing them to look at it in greater detail outside of the session, potentially even exploring it further and bringing their new insights to our next conversation. Or we could simply hold onto the link ourselves, sharing it at an appropriate point in a future session to pick things up from the point at which we left them. Time is an intriguing factor to introduce in order to take the exploration deeper.

Privacy

This, for me, raises the first challenge of digital whiteboards. Confidentiality is a really important pillar in building the trust that contributes towards the effectiveness of coaching. If I'm being coached by someone, and I lay out the difficult relationships I have with certain people and the various reasons why I'm finding them hard at the moment, I expect that information to be protected against anybody else snooping around. That's hard enough to manage when all we want is a private conversation on a video conferencing platform. Throw into the mix all of that content being captured on a digital whiteboard, being stored potentially indefinitely, and the risk landscape has just changed significantly.

The choice to store a coachee's board or not is

going to have to be made by them. That's the law, for a start, and more than that it's the right thing to do. If we're thinking about holding onto a whiteboard between sessions for the good of our coachee, let's be transparent with them about our desire to do that and the risks associated with it, and be flexible enough in our delivery to know we can delete it if they ask us to.

The learning curve

There's a second challenge as well, which comes out of how much some of these products can do. To find out the extent of that, let's open the help file for Miro,[11] one of the most popular products. When I checked just now, it named 28 different tools and 27 working styles, and has 4 chapters on exporting, 13 on sharing boards, and 5 on managing boards. The overview article for the first tool ("Cards") was 840 words long. Assuming each chapter is a similar length, that help file could easily be longer than this book.

With great power comes a great ability for things to go wrong. There are so many ways this could work itself out, it's hard to not want to talk about them all. New users might get overwhelmed by the range of buttons on display, causing them to unconsciously (or consciously!) start to sabotage the whole experience. Their view might end up in an

[11] https://miro.com/

unhelpful place, leading to confusion. They might click on something by mistake, changing an important element of the board.

I'll stop there.

The point is that a tool with the volume of capabilities some of these digital whiteboards have comes with an equivalent volume of new things to learn. With the limited amount of time we have with a coachee, using a quarter of an hour to explain which buttons do what won't feel like it's delivering the best return, and yet without it we risk derailing the whole of the session and potentially the relationship itself.

Ironically, therefore, for some coachees (and for some coaches), it might make more sense to sacrifice the bells and whistles to adopt a more stripped-back option, such as Google's Jamboard.[12] This has only eight tools in total, two of which are the default used to select items and a laser pointer. That simplicity, while no doubt frustratingly limiting for a Miro aficionado, is its beauty. The time it takes to learn how to use it is extremely short.

Alternatives

Because the best digital whiteboards are extraordinarily powerful, we're likely to find ourselves using them to do something that only uses a tiny subset of the features available. When

---

[12] https://jamboard.google.com/

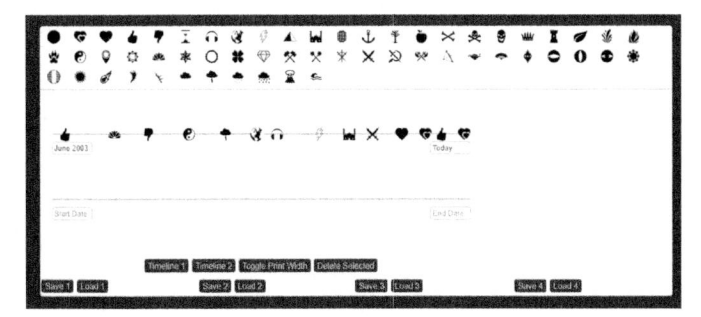

Figure 4.1 Roll for Fantasy's timeline creator

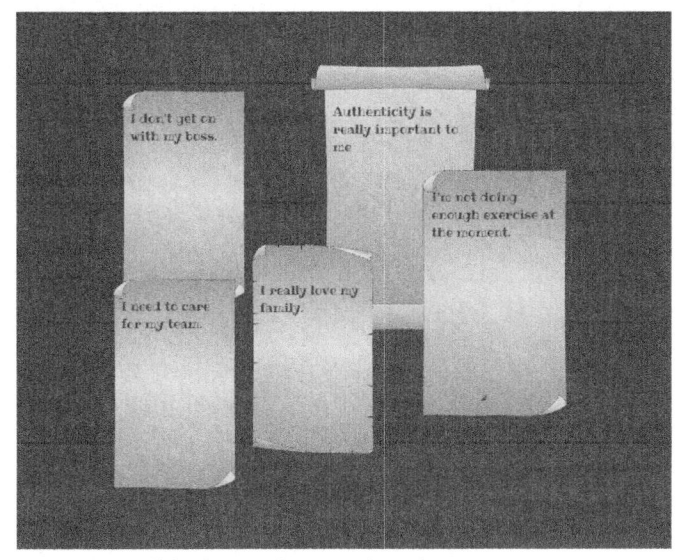

Figure 4.2 Roll for Fantasy's notice board creator

this is the case, an alternative tool might do something equally as effective in a different way.

For example, Roll for Fantasy,[13] a website designed with lovers of tabletop gaming in mind, hosts a wide variety of tools that might be

[13] https://rollforfantasy.com/

surprisingly helpful in a coaching session. There's the coat of arms generator[14] that could be used for moving shapes around, a notice board creator[15] that could be used instead of sticky notes, and a timeline creator[16] that could easily take the place of the relationship tracker described above. Each of these tools comes with straightforward, well-detailed instructions that can make the experience helpful and enjoyable.

Another option might be for a collaborative document site like Google Docs.[17] This gives us the ability to co-create a range of word processing documents, spreadsheets, and slide decks in real time. It might be perfect for a coaching session, particularly as the coachee is likely to feel a level of familiarity with it already.

---

[14] https://rollforfantasy.com/tools/coat-of-arms-creator.php

[15] https://rollforfantasy.com/tools/notice-board-creator.php

[16] https://rollforfantasy.com/tools/timeline-creator.php

[17] https://docs.google.com

5

DIGITAL PICTURE CARDS

One of the tools many coaches wouldn't have left the door without prior to the world turning upside-down in 2020 is a nice deck of picture cards. They sometimes seem to run the coaching session by themselves. Moments come along in which a coachee can't seem to express what's going on in a situation. At other times, they can tie themselves up in knots, finding themselves back again at the limiting conclusion they'd already drawn coming into the session. When we hit these problems, picture cards present a solution. Somehow, several dozen pristine photographs strewn across the floor act as a silver bullet, drawing out a stream of consciousness so insightful that the coachee feels spontaneously led to congratulate us on our superior coaching skill.

Or, at least, that's what the sales patter claims.

It's certainly true that coachees tend to find it

easy to assign meaning to images, often even without prompting. In my own coaching and supervision I've found them several times to be an extraordinary key to unlocking new ways of thinking, and I know I'm not alone.

When coaching remotely via video, this important part of some of our coaching practices might feel like it's been amputated from us. Angling the camera down and spreading some cards out on the desk in such a way that the coachee can see is an option, but it's far from ideal. Thankfully, it's not too much of a stretch to think about ways we could use technology to recreate the experience digitally, at least to a certain extent. Chucking a few dozen images onto some slides and sharing them in a coaching session is surely within the skill levels of almost every coach able to use video conferencing.

This means that the only missing ingredient for those who haven't done it yet but would want to, will have been thinking about it in the first place: You're welcome. And for those that have, but have felt sure that there must be a more elegant way to approach it, this chapter is absolutely for you.

Proven track record

The beauty about using a digital version of picture cards is how well established they are as a coaching tool. There are various versions out there supporting every flavour of coaching. Take your pick from:

- **picture cards** built around themes: landscapes, people, machines, facial expressions and ink blots to name but a few
- **process cards** that demonstrate intentional alignment with existing scientific, unscientific and pseudoscientific models
- **metaphor, values, and storytelling cards** with single words or standalone concepts on the back, providing insight and/or direction
- **self-coaching toolkits**, comprised of things like reflective questions, inspiring stories, motivational quotes, and ancient proverbs

No matter the sort of coach we feel we are, it's likely there's a deck out there for us. That should give those who haven't used them before confidence in the idea. There's no shortage of claims that such and such a product will add value to our coaching practice, so it's tempting (and right) to feel sceptical about something we might not have used before. That shouldn't be an issue for the rare coaches who haven't tried picture cards.

The digital experience in most cases is at least functionally similar to their physical counterpart in that we get to see the images, inspect the ones we're interested in, and select one or more for discussion. It's missing the embodied, tactile sensations that contribute towards them being such an enjoyable experience as part of an in-person session, so we should remain aware of that. We'll come back to it later on. We'll also loop back to the unique advantages the digital versions hold over the originals too, because this is far from being a poor replacement for an otherwise useful tool.

Delivering dopamine

One of the big reasons that coaches have always liked picture cards is the high return they offer in comparison to the low risk. Compare that equation to the experience of trying out a new coaching model, where our minds are constantly playing tricks on us as we try to remember where we are in the process, listen intently to the coachee, construct the right next question, keep an eye on the time, and actively try to ignore that niggling feeling that we're forgetting something.

The value we feel we're delivering when using picture cards is deliciously predictable. A simple question like "Which of these pictures best represents your current situation?" silently communicates to the coachee that the choice of image they're about to make has meaning. This empowers them to work that meaning out for themselves and generate insights, sometimes more quickly than we're able to do through coaching questions alone.

This rapid value creation makes the use of picture cards feel good to us. You don't need to have been a coach for a long time to know that the "aha moments" we hear about feel good to the coachee and feel just as good to us. But let's not get lost in moments of coachee insight, however good they feel. Allow us a brief sidetrack into these "aha moments".

It's worth pointing out what's happening when those "aha moments" arise. We get that feeling when we simultaneously solve a problem and notice that we've done so faster than we (perhaps unconsciously) expected ourselves to.[18] You can generate that feeling for yourself by learning almost any new skill, and there are some ways to experience it almost on demand. Any time we engage in what we might call a brain game, like a jigsaw puzzle or a cryptic crossword, we begin from a state of everything appearing at first glance to be gobbledygook. Then, a piece is found, or a clue is solved, and we find ourselves feeling ever so clever. That's why the apps that claim to train our brains feel so good, and that's the point. "Aha moments" are good at making us feel good, and interestingly less good at catalysing change, which ought to be the purpose of coaching. As Peter Hawkins summarises, "actions and insights can often be made from the left hemisphere of the neo-cortex, whereas learning that leads to transformational change involves more parts of the brain and to be enacted involves the body."[19]

[18] Dubey, R. et al. (2021). *Aha! moments correspond to metacognitive prediction errors.*

[19] Hawkins, P. (2014). The Challenge for Coaching in the 21st Century, *Organisations and People, Vol 21(4).*

Before we conclude that the last paragraph should point us away from using picture cards for insights, let's return to their purpose for us. Some coaches report that using picture cards has a tendency to generate "aha moments" more predictably than stumbling through question after question, particularly if the coachee is feeling stuck. That's helpful in one sense, giving momentum to a session and cutting through whatever negative narrative the coachee has been crafting for themselves. At the same time, it can give us false positives, making the tool a tempting safety blanket to return to in moments of need, while potentially holding our coachees back from more transformative coaching experiences. Selecting when to *not* use picture cards is just as important as reaching for them! As alternatives, those moments of breakthrough may simply come from us telling some hard truths, sitting in silence, or asking those disarming questions like "And what do you want to have happen?"

Spoiled for choice

Deciding on a digital picture card deck tool to use is a bit like being told you need to commit fully to a team in a foreign sport you don't understand. I'll explain what I mean. I'm English, and as such have been subjected to the world of football (i.e. soccer) for as long as I can remember. I therefore found it quite odd when an Israeli lady a few years ago told me in the first conversation I had with her that she was a massive fan of Hull City FC. Hull City FC is not the sort of club one expects people outside of England to have heard of. Her logic was simple: the first location she arrived at in England was Hull, so that became her football team. Naturally, she's gone on to experience the serial disappointment characteristic of so much of football. She may now regret her decision, wishing that she would have known what the team had in store before committing so wholeheartedly to it.

I share that story because we face the same choice when encountering digital picture card products. From the outside, they all essentially look the same. Then, once we've committed to one, and start to learn how it all works, we discover they all have pros and cons. Whether those are aligned to our needs or not won't become clear until we've investigated several. For that reason, let's look at four tools in this chapter. These aren't necessarily recommendations for the best, they're just examples of the different sorts of things it's possible to achieve with digital picture card tools.

Points of You

It's probably best to think of Points of You[20] first as a self-reflection tool, and it would certainly be tricky to

[20] https://www.points-of-you.com/play/

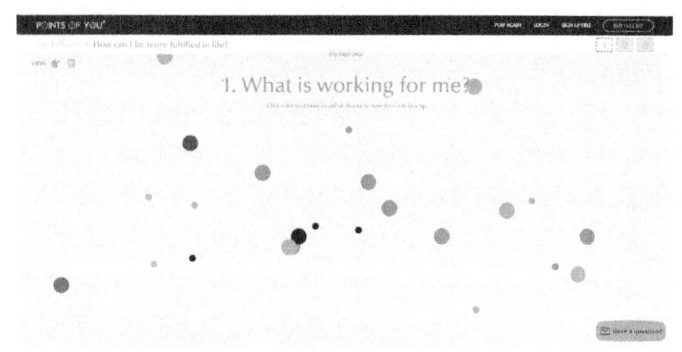

Figure 5.1 Points of You card selection screen

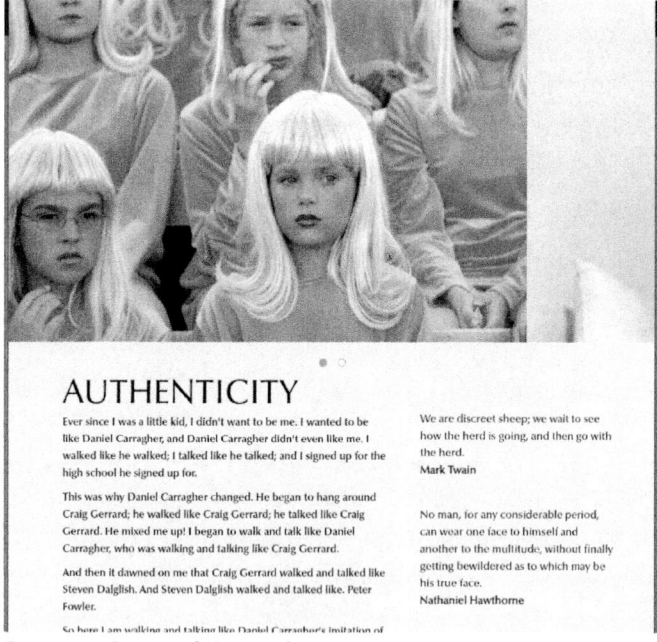

Figure 5.2 Points of You card preview

facilitate its use with a group that wasn't a team. The process is highly structured, making it less of an appealing option as a tool to pull out mid-session, but its tight control on the process will add value to those that trust it. The digital tool is free to use as a guest, and creating an account is free as well.

Upon launching it, a welcome animation plays. It's possible to skip this, which presents the downside of such a clearly thought-through process. We don't want our coaching session to be disrupted by a process that wasn't designed for them, but at the same time don't want to draw too much attention to the fact that we perhaps see what we're doing as not being a good fit for our coachee. Following the welcome animation, it's time to set up the experience. This is part of the process, selecting a topic area and focus question to contemplate. Depending on this input, it will offer three steps to respond to through the cards. These steps are set automatically by the tool, and are visible throughout. This means that if the coachee scenario aligns to one already in there, it will fit beautifully. The flip side of this is that it's more difficult to apply it haphazardly to any given coaching session.

One of the things that makes this tool particularly fun is the way the user selects a picture. There's an option to look at the pictures themselves, but the default—and more unique—method is through choosing one of the random coloured dots that drift across the screen (see Figure 5.1). Clicking on one will reveal a photograph and its associated word, with the option to see more details and browse from a selection of quotes, questions, and stories to shed more light on the situation.

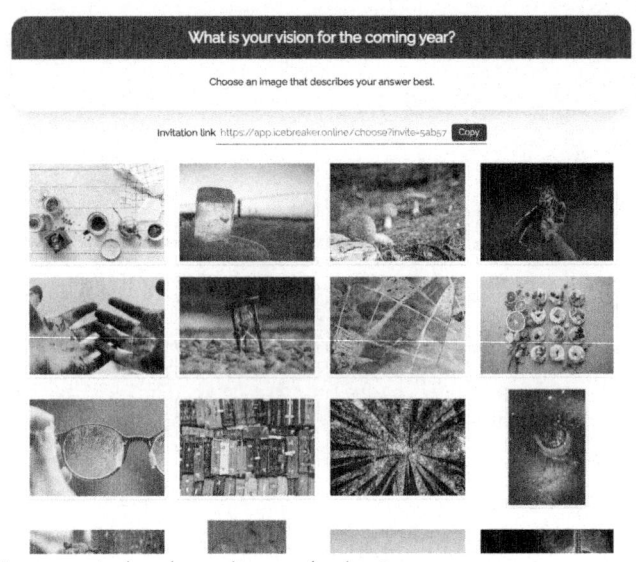

Figure 5.3 icebreaker.online card selection screen

icebreaker.online

icebreaker.online[21] is the digital version of the metaFox brand of picture cards, offering a range of high-quality photographs in various themes, along with a deck of strengths and another of values. A free account allowing limited access is available, along with a subscription-based premium account that also allows the adding of custom-built decks.

There are a couple of steps to follow to launch a session—selecting a deck and introducing a prompt—but this doesn't take very long. It generates a URL to share, and everyone involved, including the coach, selects a card. The names are displayed on the screen to give the coach full visibility over where

[21] https://app.icebreaker.online/

people are in the process. Once people have selected, the coach can then show each person's selection, one at a time, giving them a chance to share what led them to that conclusion.

Climer Cards

Climer Cards[22] have been around for a long time in physical form, and are now available digitally as well. They offer a handful of different decks at various monthly subscription prices, starting with the hand-painted originals, and also incorporating some high-quality photographs such as might be found on Unsplash or similar. Uploading custom decks is also an option.

The concept is similar to that of icebreaker.online, in that the session needs setting up in advance. This takes slightly longer, with a couple of required fields

Figure 5.4 Climer Cards card selection screen

[22]https://app.climercards.com/

that might get in the way of coaches launching it without warning in the middle of a coaching session. Each Climer Cards session can be prepared in advance and saved afterwards, with multiple rounds available each time, which makes it work quite nicely as a way to begin and end a coaching session, while maintaining the same URL. The images sit centrally on the screen, so particularly for the more panoramic photographs the purpose they serve is purely to catalyse thinking, rather than to establish an in-depth metaphor by diving into the picture. Participants enter their name and rationale manually each time they choose, and see others' entries as they appear, so facilitation of a group needs thinking through carefully, rather than the centrally-controlled experience of icebreaker.online.

deckhive

deckhive[23] is arguably a more advanced option than the previous three. There are a wide range of decks available within the tool, but none of these act in the way the others do. Rather than a set process to follow, the tool acts similarly to a digital whiteboard, allowing users to select cards from a "drawer", along with sticky notes. The cards can then be arranged on the canvas, which allows zooming in and out. Once on the screen, the cards can be duplicated, enlarged, and arranged as you wish.

[23] https://deckhive.com/

The learning curve for deckhive is unarguably greater than that of the others, and it is more expensive, but a coach wishing to have more control over the process and to access the more advanced functions will likely feel it's a good investment.

Making them effective

There are a handful of "golden rules" to any tool like this, so while we're here it's worth spending some time thinking about them. These will remain true whether we select one of the options mentioned above, or an alternative we stumble across separately as new products continue to emerge.

Always be playful

Introducing any technology tool into a coaching session risks disrupting things, because it requires a different skillset from the one normally used in coaching. A great coach might limit their capabilities by introducing technology, and a closed-off coachee might suddenly become vulnerable with the same trigger. Because technology comes naturally to some people and not to others, there's a real risk that the adult-adult relationship that coaching relies on will slip into that of parent-child unless it's managed well.

Skilfully-facilitated technology in a coaching

setting feels fun. The coachee is smiling and engaged, and the coach is in flow. Introducing pictures as a way of potentially generating new insights should feel like an adventurous experiment, and that's much easier if it's positioned as a kind of game we're playing together.

It's entirely appropriate to take some elements of coaching extremely seriously. When a coachee is struggling to reconcile their responsibilities for their team's wellbeing with the pressure they're feeling to increase their productivity, it's right to treat that as a serious issue. But just as a wedding is described as "a time of solemn commitment as well as good wishes, feasting and joy",[24] a healthy seasoning of playfulness when exploring a serious subject can sometimes be just what a coachee needs to unlock their stuck thought patterns.[25]

Always be curious

Something magical is happening when a coachee glances over the images in front of them and selects one. On any given day their choice will be different. A coach I know once told me they'd used picture cards in two consecutive sessions, where the same

[24] The Church of England (2000). *Common Worship: Marriage.* Church House Publishing

[25] Lockwood, R. & O'Connor, S. (2016): Playfulness in adults: an examination of play and playfulness and their implications for coaching, *Coaching: An International Journal of Theory, Research and Practice*

image was chosen in both. The first coachee said that the shape of a mountain in the image had amusingly reminded them of their old school teacher's haircut, who always used to give particularly wise advice. The second said the same mountain represented the challenge they were looking to overcome.

It's as if the parts of our minds that deal with cognitive processing get so fixated on the linear and rational that the solution, while sitting there somewhere, can't be found until the cognitive is bypassed. To use more accurate language, at times convergent thinking needs to make way for divergent thinking.[26] When a coach asks a question such as "Which of these pictures best represents a way forward?" divergent thinking is suddenly given permission to act, because convergent thinking has no answer for that as there is no "right" answer.

The key to unlocking these insights therefore becomes available through curiosity. What would that school teacher say if they were here right now? What made the coachee choose the mountain to represent that challenge, and not the locked door, or the stop sign, or anything else? What features does the mountain have in the picture, and what could they represent? And what features does the mountain have that aren't in the picture, only

[26] See for example DeYoung, C., Flanders, J. & Peterson, J. (2008). Cognitive Abilities Involved in Insight Problem Solving: An Individual Differences Model, *Creativity Research Journal*, 20:3, 278-290

existing in the coachee's mind? These sorts of questions are inherently irrational. The mountain doesn't truly represent anything, it's just a picture. At the same time, it captures the truth of the coachee's situation more perfectly than words alone can. That irrationality is precisely what the divergent thinking needs, in order to be let loose.

The coachee's meaning is the meaning

This means that we need to follow where the coachee is going more than ever with this sort of exercise. There's a lot of talk about being non-directive in coaching, and when we're exploring something using the coachee's "metaphor landscape"[27] it's essential that we don't make assumptions by imposing our own interpretations onto what they're noticing.

At times this will mean accepting something truly ridiculous in the moment, for the sake of supporting the coachee in pursuing whatever their mind has done to get them to that point. In fact, if we do that well, we'll likely conclude that it's much less ridiculous than we thought at first.

---

[27] See Tompkins, P. and Lawley, J. (2000). *Metaphors in Mind: Transformation Through Symbolic Modelling*, London: Developing Company Press

Who—or what—is the coachee?

The way to use these tools is different when using them with an individual rather than with a group, so it's worth playing out our own scenarios around when we will use them, and how. The value they bring in accelerating insight often comes from slowing down and reflecting on the pictures. Because a group needs a lot more time management, this needs thinking through properly. Each tool will deal with this differently, so we need to make sure to get some practice in before introducing it to a more sensitive coachee situation for the first time.

This is particularly important when comparing how the experience is different between an individual, a team, and a group. With an individual that curiosity looks at times like getting sidetracked, as mentioned in chapter 3. That perspective needs to be carefully managed with a team, because those wanting to dive down a rabbit hole may actually be sabotaging the process, however unwittingly. With a group it should be avoided almost entirely, due to the fact that others may well be waiting for their turn in the limelight.

Given the different techniques the tools use to offer image choices to the coachee and facilitate feedback, we will likely end up with different preferences depending on the circumstance. As we're reflecting on this and our varied approaches, let's constantly remind ourselves that a well-designed slide deck may well be a perfectly decent workaround.

Advantages of digital picture cards

One of the best things about using picture cards in person is the tactile experience it offers, taking us away from the word-filled conversation and towards something different, more embodied in nature. Current technology puts that experience a step or two further away than we can recreate digitally (to a certain extent—more in chapters 11 and 12), but offers us some unique advantages that physical picture cards can't; let's call out three.

Firstly, we need to take special care of physical picture cards. It just isn't as nice to look at a pile of filthy, dog-eared postcards as it is to look at a pristine, new set. One spilt cup of coffee, and that's a deck of cards rendered pretty much unusable in future. Digital cards can't get damaged that way.

Secondly, physical picture card decks are simultaneously one item and several, illustrating the magical capacity human beings have to think at different levels of abstraction. The problem with this is that one coachee might pick up a card and like it so much they inadvertently hold onto it at the end of a session, deeming it unavailable for the next person. That also works in a group setting, where two people might want to inspect the same card. Digital cards avoid all of that by only existing virtually, meaning they can appear however we want them to, and can retain that state even between coaching sessions. Not only can individual digital cards never be lost, their relationships with one another can be saved, to return to in a future session in the same way that we saw with digital whiteboards.

Finally, physical picture cards are much less sanitary than we'd like them to be. A coachee won't think twice about picking up every card in view, and then the next might do exactly the same thing. How comfortable would we be telling a coachee how many people have touched those cards before them? Digital cards are just about as hygienic as it's possible to get.

Introducing joy

Having said all of that, let's not lose sight of the role these cards can play in a coaching session. Whether physical or digital, they act as a helpful disrupter to a purely verbal conversation, shifting thinking and generating a different sort of energy. For some coachees—and some coaches—this will be an extremely natural new segment of a session, while for others it might feel uncomfortable at first. In any case, it will inject a forced change of approach. This is helpful in many situations, and more often than not will act as a catalyst for greater pleasure in the coaching process, including the further embedding of new ways of thinking following each session.

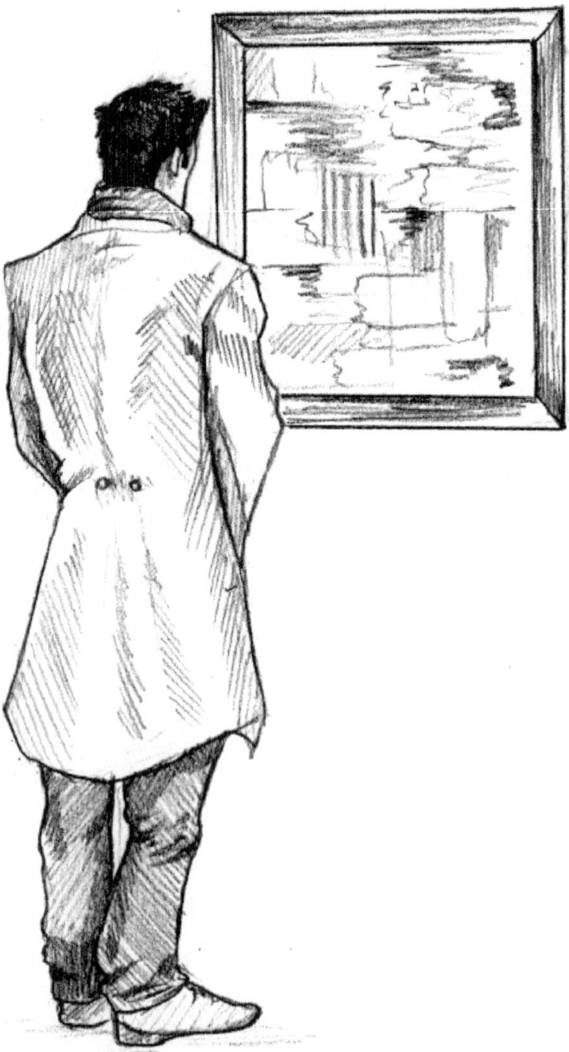

6

AI-GENERATED ARTWORK

Having explored what can happen when introducing a visual stimulus into a coaching session, it's worth taking that a step further. It's one thing to take an existing image and use it as a catalyst for greater insight, and quite another to empower a coachee to create one for themselves.

When delivering in-person coaching, some coaches have been known to have a lump of clay to hand, or some coloured pipe cleaners, LEGO bricks, or a selection of pens and paper.[28] These are great for allowing a coachee to express themselves, and offer a different route to unlocking insights from the

[28] For a short and interesting look at some other examples of creativity in coaching, see Falato, D. (2012). *Research Paper: How Using Art Making as a Coaching Tool Supports Client Learning*. Retrieved from: https://coachcampus.com/coach-portfolios/research-papers/dawn-falato-how-using-art-making-as-a-coaching-tool-supports-client-learning/

picture cards option. But they come with a bit of a health warning:

- They can take time to create, replacing valuable coaching questions and thinking time with arts and crafts; perhaps enjoyable and certainly of use in its own right, and equally certainly difficult to manage for most coaches
- Coachees who do not feel like gifted creatives can become frustrated with their lack of skill and become distracted from the purpose of the activity
- Coachees who *do* feel like gifted creatives can get lost in the quality of what they're producing and ironically also become distracted from the purpose of the activity

This chapter brings good news. It's possible to create something that uniquely captures a coachee's issue in a creative, visual manner, without the exercise of the creation process getting in the way. The solution is artwork generated by artificial intelligence (AI), based on inputs from the coachee.

Unique for one coachee in one session

The Barnum Effect is what happens when an individual looks at something that could apply to anyone, and believes it applies specifically to them.

The message in a fortune cookie telling the reader they will be grateful for the next challenge they face might feel eerily accurate for some. As a result, however, this tendency can lead the sceptical among us to ignore even the good impacts of believing that the message should be applied to us, and that's true for coachees too.

The beauty of AI-generated artwork is how it entirely eliminates a perception of the Barnum Effect. A challenge a coachee might raise—even silently—with the picture cards of the last chapter is that the mountain that stands out so much to them, to hark back to the example we used, equally stood out to the previous coachee, and therefore cannot possibly be as full of meaning as they assumed at first. Because the coaching is non-directive, that fact really isn't important. If the coachee gains insights from looking at it, that's all that matters. It's like the way a person drawing a tarot card at random might benefit from an insight. The point is not whether or not tarot is "real", it's that humans are meaning makers, and any way we can accelerate insights is good within the context of a coaching session.

That criticism cannot be levelled at AI-generated artwork. With these products, a machine dynamically produces a brand new image based on two inputs. Firstly, a large dataset of existing artworks provide a set of guide rails for the art,[29][30] indicating a style that will work. Secondly, a text-

[29] Flaherty, D. (2020). *Artistic approaches to machine learning.* Queensland University of Technology, Masters Thesis

based input provides content it attempts to then create from, shaping what appears in the finished image.

This means two things. Firstly, the image in question doesn't exist until the moment the coachee sees it, and stops existing as soon as the window is closed. If the coachee doesn't want anyone else in the world, including the coach, to see their artwork, that can happen. That takes confidentiality to a new high, and removes the potential nagging doubt in the mind of a coachee when selecting a picture card: Does everybody choose this picture?

Secondly, it's undeniable that the picture relates to the coachee's topic. A coachee in some cases might feel shoehorned into selecting one of a limited deck of images. It's true that some decks have been carefully designed to lead towards a particular outcome; one deck that can be fun to use is simply a selection of different designs of door! In contrast, this AI-generated artwork has been especially made for them. The coachee is not free to excuse themselves by thinking "This picture of a mountain doesn't *really* relate to the relationship between me and my line manager!" No, when using

---

[30] To see the sort of original fine art that was produced based on analysis of 5,000 impressionist paintings in the public domain, see Gonsalves, R. A. (2021). *GANscapes: Using AI to Create New Impressionist Paintings*. Retrieved from: https://towardsdatascience.com/ganscapes-using-ai-to-create-new-impressionist-paintings-d6af1cf94c56

this sort of tool, that's the only thing it relates to, because it's the only textual content it's been generated from.

Be unreasonably curious

This is different from the way picture cards are used. With a picture card, we need to respect the coachee's meaning as they interpret the image. With an AI artwork tool, we need to push this out even further, entirely letting go of any other meaning altogether. The tool has created something that would not have existed were it not for the coachee working with us in this way today!

Indeed, and not to turn this into some mystical experience, providing precisely the same input 100 times would produce 100 different outputs, so the particular image the coachee is viewing in this moment is extremely special. While the coachee might not feel a liking for the image when they first see it, they cannot escape from the fact that it doesn't relate to anyone or anything else. They have no excuses to avoid parts of the picture they feel don't apply, because those parts only exist thanks to their prompt.

Because the creations we're working with in these instances only exist for the coachee in this particular session, we have licence to be even more curious about what meaning the image might hold than we might be with one of the images from the previous chapter. Rather than the image having some other natural meaning that we're somehow manipulating for the purposes of today's session, with these tools the image's only meaning is the input we gave it.

Imagine for a moment that the input typed in is "I need to get better at public speaking". If the image appears to the coachee to look like a mountain, while this interpretation may be valid, it cannot act as an excuse to avoid discussing the topic at hand. The mountain—if that is what it is—absolutely must represent something of meaning to the coachee's need to improve in public speaking. We have permission to press in, while the stock images can more easily be brushed aside by the coachee.

One way we can see this in action is through asking the silly questions. Asking what a particular mark or smudge represents is valid, because it has only been introduced thanks to the coachee's input.

An emerging technology

This sort of technology has only existed for a few years. It isn't purely creative, but instead uses a large dataset of images deemed to be correct to create boundaries within which the tool makes something new. Because the technology's so new, at times the artworks might be far from perfect, and will vary widely in what they try to do. Let's look at a

AI-GENERATED ARTWORK 93

Figure 6.1: Art created in WOMBO Dream from the prompt "Inclusive leadership"

selection of tools, bearing in mind the fact that new options are becoming available all the time.

WOMBO Dream

WOMBO Dream[31] has both mobile apps and a browser-based option you can use on a desktop PC. It doesn't need an account to make it work and requires no setup time. Navigating to the page and sharing the link with a coachee is all you need to do to use it live in a session. The user interface is simple; the coachee types in a prompt of up to 100 characters and selects an art style, and the tool generates an image in 10-15 seconds. The outputs tend towards the abstract, which is probably more helpful. AI tools that attempt to create more realistic art are sometimes accompanied by unattractive and distracting quirks.

Hotpot

Hotpot creates a range of AI tools, including their AI Art Maker.[32] This tool again doesn't need an account, although some options (such as the ability to make the generated artwork private) are restricted to paying customers. The interface is simple, with the same options as with WOMBO

[31] https://www.wombo.art/

[32] https://hotpot.ai/art-maker

Dream, with the added ability to introduce your own image into the design process.

The time it takes might act as a blocker for most coaches using this in a live coaching session—several minutes at a minimum—but it only needs a change in approach. The way to use this is therefore to set the process going when the coachee sets a topic for the session, and leave it running in the background while the conversation moves forward. At an opportune moment later on in the session, we can bring in the image to shed some more light on what's been discussed so far.

The outputs for Hotpot feel a bit more varied than WOMBO Dream in terms of style. It comes with options to make the image photorealistic and to use a simpler art style, which some coachees might particularly appreciate depending on their preferences and the topics they're discussing.

NightCafe Creator

NightCafe Creator[33] is a nicely-designed tool that works in a similar way to WOMBO Dream. It doesn't need an account, but creating one gives access to previous creations. It operates on a credit system: five free credits per day, with additional credits earned for certain activities or for a price. The front page is extremely simple, and some more advanced features are hidden behind a pleasing

---

[33]https://creator.nightcafe.studio/

"More options" button.

The image can be "evolved" after it has been created, and a couple of the options make it feel more widely applicable (such as a switch that can make it more abstract or cohesive), and it takes a couple of minutes for it to run—much closer in time to WOMBO Dream than Hotpot's tool. For providing a bit more control (or perceived control) in the hands of the coachee, NightCafe Creator feels like a good mix to help generate an image that can be taken away for further reflection.

Figure 6.2 Art created in NightCafe Creator from the prompt "Inclusive leadership"

Capturing the memory

As with the picture cards, a coachee may want something to take away with them to remember what's been discussed. Because the images created through these tools are dynamically generated only for this session, this needs paying particular attention to. If the window is closed, it's gone forever. For this reason, it's worth getting into the habit of copying the image as soon as it's created, and saving it in a separate document as a safety net. Depending on the tool, we can download a high-resolution version of the image, and even order a print on canvas. This sort of output might be perfect for certain coachees, as reminders of particularly meaningful insights they want to be constantly reminded of.

PEACHES AND MOONSHINE
THE RED LADY CRIES OUT
IN A CRYSTAL WILLOW
AM I MISSING GREEN?

7

CREATIVE WRITING

If the last two chapters have outlined how visual stimuli can activate divergent thinking to find new solutions to unsolved problems, this chapter will do the same thing but make use of words instead of pictures. When I first came across this concept, it appeared to me to be confusing; isn't it the case that images work in coaching specifically because they remove words from the equation?

In a sense that's true, and yet there's surprising value hidden in what these products offer us. Partly, as we'll see, the way we'll be using words here forces us into more creative spaces in our minds. In addition, the use of words introduce constraints that can actually be helpful in creativity, as we'll explore right now.

Enforce limitations

We've all experienced analysis paralysis when buying a gift. All we want is to buy a friend a nice present, and yet the endless possibilities of the internet that hint that the perfect gift lies on the next page of the search engine only reveal to us that whatever we choose will be less than perfect. This "paradox of choice"[34] shows that it's much more satisfying and pragmatic to be presented with the choice: Would they prefer a box of chocolates or a personalised mug?

This idea of constraints is true when it comes to innovative thinking, too. Trying to innovate with endless choices can stop good thinking, whereas some clear limitations can make it that bit simpler to come up with new ideas. We see this with organisations all the time. Some of the most innovative organisations got to a certain size, and then lost their innovative edge. Bobby Gruenewald, CEO of YouVersion, creator of one of the most downloaded and used mobile apps, goes so far as to say: "I'd argue that if we aren't facing any natural constraints, we should create some."[35]

This has an immediate practical application in the

---

[34]Schwartz, B. (2004). *The Paradox of Choice: Why More Is Less*. Harper Perennial

[35]Gruenewald, B. (2015). *The Innovation Equation: Problems + Limitations = Innovation*. Retrieved from: https://outreachmagazine.com/features/5656-the-innovation-equation.html

tool we'll look at in this chapter, Magnetic Poetry.[36] When I was a child, our family was given a box full of words printed onto little magnets that you could move around on the fridge, forming nonsense poems. That product is now available in digital format, for a bit of mindless fun in a low-energy moment.

And as a powerful coaching tool.

How is that connected to limitations? The box of words doesn't contain every word in the dictionary, and the digital version is even more restricted (unless you press the "Load more words" button, which we should forbid our coachees from doing). That restriction makes it usable. Ask a coachee to write a poem about an issue, and there's a good chance their instinct will be to just say that they can't do it. Most people aren't used to writing poems, so the idea of doing it without warning, particularly in a time-bound setting like a coaching session, will be unhelpfully disruptive for some.

The limited choice of words makes it simpler to get that engagement. Because the words are there, the need to think up the best words is gone, and there's a guarantee that the poem will be awful, taking away the pressure to perform as well.

In practice

To illustrate this, why not head over to the website

[36]http://magneticpoetryplayonline.com/

now and compile a quick poem about your reflections on this book so far? I'll write one here for you as an example:

> *Smooth friends together*
> *Shadow diamonds from spring moonlight*
> *Like fast men boil & beat as if mad*
> *Our shine is here*
> *Asking*
> *But how*

There was meaning in each new line as I pulled that together, it really didn't take long, and I hope it illustrates what can happen with this tool. We can see simultaneous clarity and ambiguity, deep meaning communicated through gibberish.

It's in this that we experience the crossover with the previous chapters. The coachees create a poem that gains meaning as they progress. They're forced out of the left-brain, rational, linear, convergent thinking and into a more present state. Their minds make connections between the jumble of words in front of them and whatever spaghetti of ideas they have in their minds, bringing new insights and perspectives.

Other digital creative writing tools

Of course, creative writing is much more than simply poetry, and Magnetic Poetry is only one approach. Here are a few others we might want to consider to add some spice to our coaching.

Fantasy Name Generators

Fantasy Name Generators,[37] like its sister site Roll for Fantasy, which we saw in chapter 4, were created with tabletop roleplaying games (RPGs) in mind. In an RPG, the person running the game is responsible for generating a setting and storyline that is reasonably believable, allowing the players to explore and be immersed in the fictional environment. This is surprisingly difficult, particularly when it comes to naming places and people. Many RPG players are used to encountering a Boblin the Goblin from time to time.

Fantasy Name Generators, and other sites like it, will create random, yet believable location and character names at the push of a button. It hosts more than 1,400 name and description generators, all of which are accessible through generous menus that fill the top of the screen. For example, I've just asked it to give me some Irish names. These are the first four it gave me (two male, two female):

---

[37] https://www.fantasynamegenerators.com/

- Arthur Tully
- Robert MacWard
- Abigail Mulligan
- Zoe O'Sheehan

Believably Irish names, and entirely random. This can be helpfully used with a coachee looking to explore a complex situation, through introducing fictional personalities or places. On the surface, this could act as a powerful way to reveal unconscious bias; when you read the name "Arthur Tully", what sort of person appeared, unbidden, in your mind's eye? More deeply, that natural tendency we have to generate quite well-developed characters when all we know is their name could be used to help a coachee play out a challenging scenario they have coming up, such as an interview.

Other parts of the website are much more adventurous, offering randomised character backstories, for example. Here's the opening line of an example it's just created. Using something like this with a coachee acts in a similar way to the

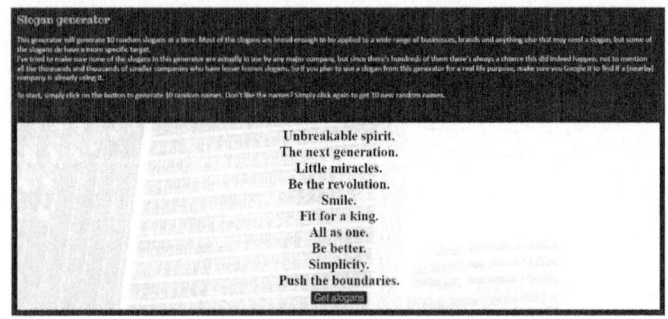

Figure 7.1 The slogan generator from Fantasy Name Generators

assigning of meaning we were looking at in the previous chapter.

> *He's happy, intelligent, humorous and perhaps a little too selfish. But what'd you expect from somebody with his position.*

I'd thoroughly recommend a browse across the site, with a curious eye open to how different aspects might lend themselves to a coaching session.

Fantasy Name Generators is free to use, and doesn't need an account.

Rytr

Rytr[38] is one of a raft of AI text generators that takes some input and turns it into a range of different text outputs. For example, if I type the input "How to increase my resilience", select the tone as "Inspirational", and the use case as writing a blog post, these are the opening lines:

> *Resilience is the ability to bounce back from adversity. It's about finding a way to get through tough times, and it doesn't happen overnight. In order to increase your resilience, you need to work on your mental health and*

---

[38] https://rollforfantasy.com/

think about what makes you happy. You also need some tips on managing stress in your life so it doesn't get too overwhelming.

Perhaps not the most creative few sentences, but as a catalyst for thinking around the subject, I've seen much worse. It's disconcertingly similar to a lot of content we find ourselves reading online. If a coachee is looking for a solution to a particular issue and we're conscious we don't want to accidentally step into becoming too directive, those few sentences —and it's possible to click "Continue Ryting" for more!—might be enough to encourage their own thinking on the subject. Other approaches and other tools offer a wide range of output styles.

A free Rytr account will let you generate up to 5,000 characters per month, and paid plans allow for more.

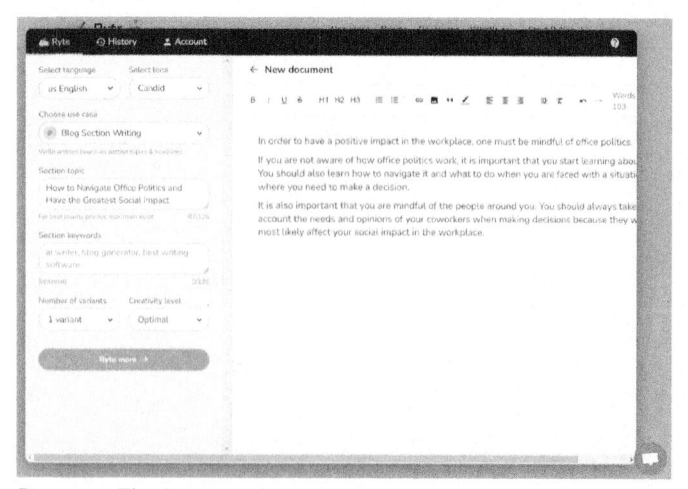

Figure 7.2 The Rytr interface

Figure 7.3 AnswerThePublic output from the input "public speaking"

AnswerThePublic

AnswerThePublic[39] describes itself as a search listening tool, analysing Google search activity and reporting back the search terms people are using related to an input we provide. The concept is easy to understand, presented in attractive visual ways with branches reaching out from the core word(s), and downloadable as a spreadsheet as well.

It takes less than a minute to run, so is manageable live in a coaching session, and the sorts of outputs it offers for the input "good leaders" are:

- Are good leaders born or made?
- Do introverts make good leaders?
- Why good leaders make you safe
- Good leaders lose with grace

I would hope that these are no more insightful than the sort of thoughts we might come up with

[39] https://answerthepublic.com/

ourselves, but that's not the point. The power is in a coachee activating the tool themselves, identifying which of the search terms resonate the most, and either reflecting on those or—potentially more helpfully—tapping into some metacognition around what it was about those that stood out.

The tool can be used for free, but there's a daily limit based on the amount of traffic the site is experiencing, so it might be risky to run it live in a coaching session. Paid accounts are available, allowing for unlimited searches and a range of other features.

Give it time

The foundation of curiosity, of course importantly present within all coaching interactions, remains important when dealing with text-based digital tools. For the same reasons as we looked at with regard to the use of images, activating curiosity around why a particular word choice seemed to make sense when all available words—to a certain extent—would have been valid can offer enticing insights.

An important difference between the use of pictures and that of words is in the time pressure we should be introducing. For images, the coachee's gut reaction can be very helpful, so inducing a need to choose quickly can be a good tool to draw out to create momentum. When selecting words however, many coachees will need time for them to form in their minds. Allowing more space might allow a coachee to understand how that word might apply, and identify wordplays that trigger more creative thinking.

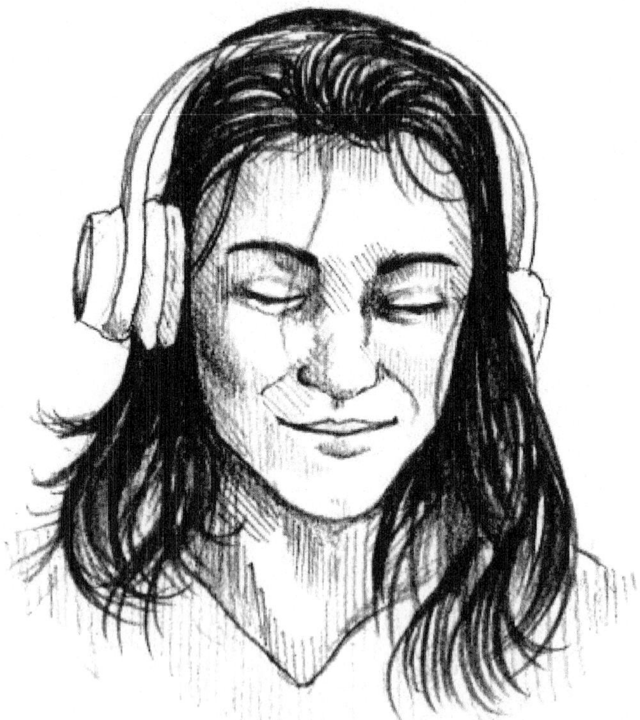

8

TECHNOLOGY FOR MULTISENSORY COACHING

We've looked at several creative tools that require a visual element. Aware that some coachees prefer to not see themselves as particularly visual and some are blind, preventing them from benefiting in the same way from these tools, let's take some time to explore something that doesn't use any visuals, tapping instead into sound.

Sound is a core part of the human experience for most people, and despite the dominance of imagery in our media, sound is extremely powerful in its ability to reproduce reality. I was watching a television programme only yesterday in which the sound effect of a vibrating phone caused me to fish mine out of my pocket, despite me not feeling anything! The moving pictures on a TV have never caused me to do something like that. Sound is unique in the fact that it is ubiquitous—the smartphone became mainstream essentially due to the combining of phone and music player—and good quality sounds are also deeply convincing, while we're much more easily able to visually differentiate between fact and fiction.

This particular meeting point creates an attractive foundation for a wide range of use cases in coaching, from which I'll highlight one particular tool and a selection of applications.

MyNoise

MyNoise[40] is a website hosting more than 200 dynamically generated soundscapes, including noise blockers, binaural beats, emergent music and sound effects among many others. I like it because the sound quality is the highest I've found, its graphic interface is straightforward, the choice is constantly growing, the owner seems switched on with the right intent, and the value for money is better than you can imagine. It's possible to use almost all of the soundscapes for free, and with a very small payment we get lifetime access to a range of additional features.

The page for each soundscape includes around ten stems, each representing a different band of sound frequencies. Each individual stem generates

[40] https://mynoise.net/

TECHNOLOGY FOR MULTISENSORY COACHING 113

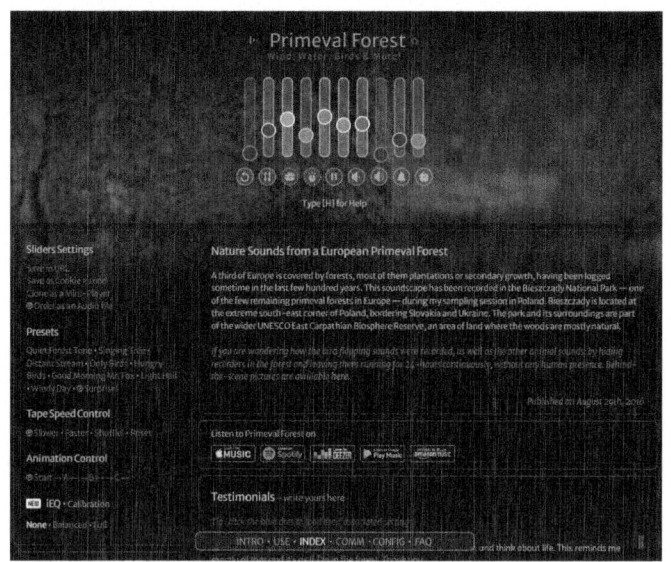

Figure 8.1 The MyNoise interface

sounds that are carefully designed to be both pleasant to listen to and not distracting, and when they come together they can achieve all manner of outcomes. Based on research, certain sound selections will aid in focus, or relaxation, or creativity.[41] And the high level of customisation available within each soundscape allows us to produce a personalised auditory experience that I've never seen anywhere else.

Why not head over there right now? When you have a chance to explore its depths, you'll quickly

[41]Mehta, R., Zhu, R. (Juliet), & Cheema, A. (2012). Is Noise Always Bad? Exploring the Effects of Ambient Noise on Creative Cognition. *Journal of Consumer Research, 39(4)*, 784–799

find a couple you like to simply have playing in the background while you work or read, and let's have a look at some ways you might find it helpful in a coaching session.

Mindful moments

It's nice sometimes to imagine a world in which coachees arrive to every coaching session fully present and ready to take the reins. Of course, this probably wouldn't be any fun in practice, and we live in a reality in which this isn't the case. Particularly when a coachee is in back-to-back video calls, leaping directly into a coaching model isn't always the most helpful way to begin a coaching session, so a few moments to still the soul and enter fully into our time together can be an effective investment of time.

For some coachees, simply being asked to sit quietly for a moment, taking a couple of deep breaths, and actively laying aside the busyness of the day might be enough. For others, whether that's because of the environment they're in, their current state of mind, or their natural traits, they might need a helping hand. A carefully selected soundscape, perhaps with input from the coachee, might be precisely the sort of thing they're looking for. We can share a link, or share our screen with audio, and off we go.

Even for those coachees who try to directly

counter these sorts of exercises (you know the sort, they tend to say things like "I just don't get any of this hippy nonsense"), the experience of closing one's eyes and being transported to the middle of a tropical rainforest is relatively universal in the way it makes virtually stepping away from the desk immediately accessible.

Try it yourself. Offer a coachee a single minute of simply listening to the raindrops bouncing off the deep green leaves, and they'll invariably open their eyes feeling more present, and probably wanting a longer time there next session.

Visioning

An exercise some coachees find helpful is that of imagining a desirable future state. The theory goes that spending time exploring our ideal self induces a psychophysiological state that makes achieving complex goals that bit more natural.[42] But a vivid imagination is something that comes more naturally to some than others, so it stands to reason that some coachees are disadvantaged when it comes to this sort of exercise. If a soundscape will help a coachee who finds that skillset less easy to access visualise their goals, we should be ready to make it available to them.

For example, a coachee might answer the

[42]Passarelli, A. (2015). Vision-based coaching: optimizing resources for leader development. *Frontiers in Psychology* 6:412.

question "Where do you see yourself in ten years if everything goes to plan?" with "Lying on a beach somewhere would be nice!" Perhaps that's an uninspired, generic, and unrealistic response. Or perhaps it's precisely the sort of motivational vision they need. Using a beach soundscape will help them to visualise it that much better, and that remains true if their answer was "In the boardroom", "In Senegal", or "In a monastery". Donning the headphones, immersing themselves in the environment, and making this vision come alive for them will allow them to analyse it more deeply, increasing their self-awareness in the process and catalysing the behaviour change that will get them there, if that's what makes most sense.

Tips for use

Let's start with the obvious. While MyNoise will feel intuitive to some, there's a lot going on. Trying to work all that out live in a session with a coachee is going to be less than ideal. Becoming familiar with the interface, a dozen or so of the soundscapes, and some of the more advanced options will enable us to use it efficiently and effectively in a non-distracting way.

The practicalities around sharing the sounds with a coachee are as simple as sharing the screen, making sure that we're sharing the audio as well as the picture. On this point, it's my view that the audio interface, particularly if we're manipulating it in real time, can prove a bit of a distraction to a coachee. It's probably therefore most effective to share a blank slide while playing the sound in the background. Some video conferencing platforms allow this to work better than others, so running a test or two before bringing it out in anger will be a good idea.

As a general rule, we will want to provide some instructions and then mute ourselves before launching the sound. Some video platforms want only one audio channel playing at a time, and so our voice, as valuable as we might like to think it is, will interfere with the experience rather than adding to it.

Finally, let's return to where we ended the previous chapter. Soundscapes are another tool that reward patience and silent curiosity on our part. Uninterrupted immersion in the space is what's likely to bring the insight, so we should give the coachee as much time as possible, using the overall volume down control (keyboard shortcut J when we have MyNoise open) to subtly remove the sound and indicate that it's time to return to the conversation.

Alternatives

A Soft Murmur

For those needing a simpler option, A Soft Murmur[43] offers a stripped-down interface without any of the more advanced features offered by MyNoise. As a streamlined way to introduce sounds into coaching without the distractions of the more advanced elements, A Soft Murmur will be a good option. The pros of the simplicity bring with them the cons of a lack of customisation and the risk of a coachee noticing repeated sounds much more than with MyNoise, so as with every other product it will be worth experimenting to see which feels the best fit.

Imaginary Soundscape

This offers something quite different and at times unexpected. Imaginary Soundscape[44] uses audio as an input to inject something different into a coaching session. It's an AI tool that uses a bank of sound recordings to respond dynamically to an image present on the screen. You can use Google Street View to travel to whichever locations you might want to, or you can upload your own image.

[43] https://asoftmurmur.com/

[44] https://imaginarysoundscape.net/

The sounds are wildly unpredictable, sometimes absolutely nailing it, and at other times providing unexpected disruptors. While experimenting with it, I travelled to central London and was greeted with the sounds of people talking and slow-moving traffic. Perfect. I then went to my parents' home in rural Yorkshire, where the tool presented me with what sounded like an emergency services call about a dangerous fire. It wasn't a pleasant experience. With certain coachees in certain situations, a playfulness might be as much permission as you need to do something unpredictable, and perhaps that would be precisely the right thing to do. I don't think you need me to point out that others wouldn't respond so well. As fun as some of these tools might be, our professional responsibilities and codes of ethics are more important.

Endel

Endel[45] is an AI-powered generator of music, rather than soundscapes. It plays a small selection of semi-abstract music based around key objectives, each one personalised, adaptive, and based on neuroscience.[46] The soundscapes on offer are

[45] https://endel.io/

[46] Haruvi, A. et al. (2021). Modeling The Effect of Background Sounds on Human Focus Using Brain Decoding Technology. Retrieved from: https://www.biorxiv.org/content/10.1101/2021.04.02.438269v3

designed for things like relaxation, study, movement (responding to a phone's accelerometer or a wearable), and sleep, and each is accompanied by an animation. The interface is as simple as they come, and there is no customisation once the music has started playing. That's a strength in that it's one button press and we're on our way, and it's also a

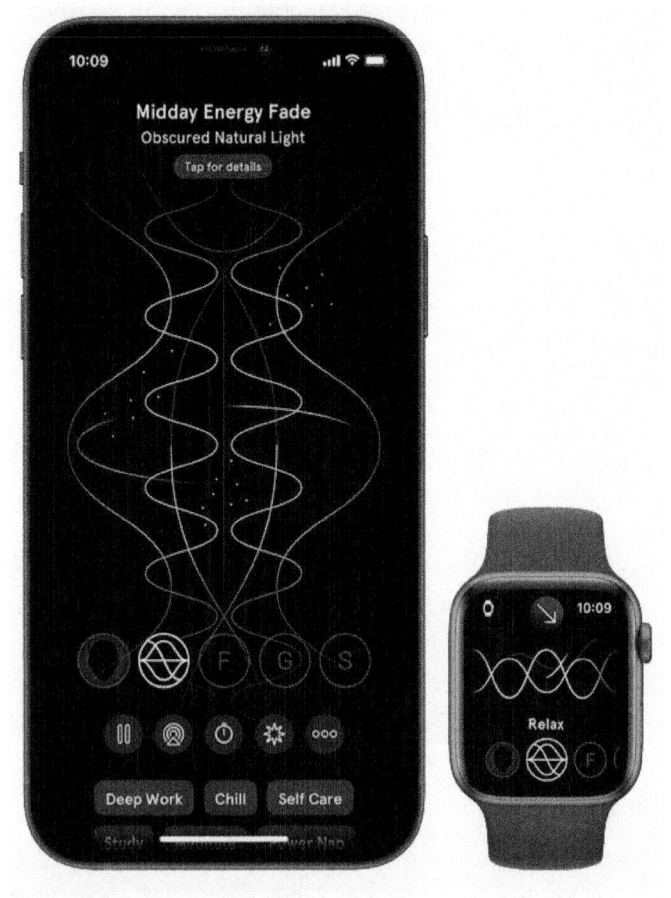

Figure 8.2 A musical soundscape playing on Endel's iPhone and Apple Watch apps

weakness in that the sound can change quite significantly over time, and apart from a single "reframe" button there's no way to manually edit it.

The nature of these as slowly emerging soundscapes might make Endel difficult to use live in coaching sessions in practice. The recommended minimum length of time to listen is 15 minutes, so a decent chunk of a session needs to be sacrificed in order to get maximum benefit from the tool.

Accessing some pre-recorded soundscapes is straightforward enough on their YouTube channel. The Android mobile app is free and comes with four emergent soundscapes, with the rest accessible through a subscription. It's also accessible through its website, for Apple devices including the Apple Watch, and through voice commands via Alexa.

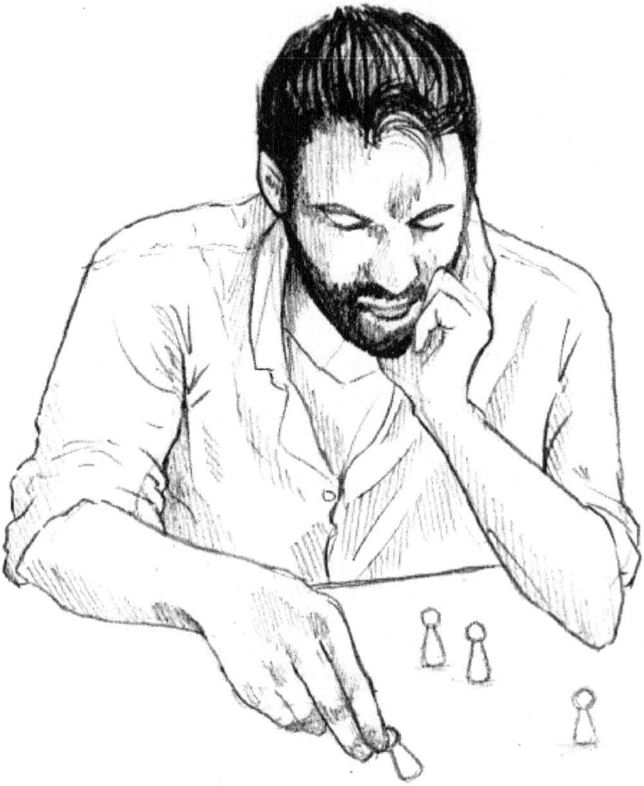

9

CONSTELLATIONS

The idea of using objects to represent people and concepts that a coachee is experiencing in their life is a well-established tool in many coaches' toolkits. Commonly referred to as constellations, objects are arranged in such a way that their (relative) location and visual appearance represent the map the coachee has built in their head. This allows them to crystallise what they've been thinking, experiment with different perspectives, and explore what might be possible.

There's no doubt that constellations exercises are profoundly helpful. The representations generated make this sort of tool a true aid to any coach working with a coachee, as they try to navigate the systems they interact with. This is becoming increasingly important. Coaching happening inside an organisation is often systemic by design, and coachees are aware of their need for growth in this area. I know this is true anecdotally; "office politics" is a topic that's come up at least as much as any other in my own coaching and among those coaches I've spoken to about it. And the data backs this up. Digital coaching provider Ezra analyses which sort of content coaches share with their coachees, and "Operating in the Matrix" (office politics by another name) is one of the top three most popular topics shared overall. In the first half of 2022 it was the most shared topic.

The original root of these tools comes from the therapeutic practice of "family constellations",[47] in which an individual will select a group of people to each represent someone in their family, positioning them spatially and in a stance that best represents the way they see them within their internal map. This typically takes place with a group of up to 20 people, so a smaller-scale version evolved that could be used in 1:1 settings.

The visualisation of a constellation naturally supports systemic coaching through making the coachee's inner understanding as tangible as possible, allowing for alternative perspectives to be taken. In particular, taking in the system as a whole can bring a new sense of insight. A coachee might discover that one part of the system simply isn't aware of another, or that the perceptions they've

---

[47] See for example Mahr, A. (1998). *Ein Plädoyer für's Innehalten — Systemische Familienaufstellungen bei Trennung und Scheidung.*

developed aren't helpful to support positive change.

Products designed precisely for this sort of exercise exist. One example would be the physical version of Coaching Constellations, in which smooth, wooden avatars are placed on a circular mat on a table to represent the system. Alternative in-person approaches have included toy people such as LEGO or Playmobil characters, nondescript items such as buttons, and matryoshka dolls.

Given the value of these insights, there should be no surprise that digital options have sprouted up, allowing for constellations to be created using technology. For example, there's Coaching Constellations Online,[48] a downloadable pack of images that together recreate the official Coaching Constellations product, designed explicitly for use in coaching sessions.

Considering the coachee experience

This history as a physical, highly tactile experience introduces an interesting dynamic when we approach the technology, in a similar way to the one we'll experience if we begin to use digital picture cards. Depending on our preferences, the technology will be designed to either replicate the physical experience as closely as possible, or make it as digitally friendly as possible—but it can't be both!

[48] https://coachingconstellations.com/online-facilitation-kit/

This is not to say that one is better than the other, simply that they're not the same. We therefore ought to think carefully about which will suit us and our coachees.

Let me give you a nerdy example of this in practice. In the 1980s and 90s, a new genre of book appeared: Interactive fiction. This was popularised through the *Choose Your Own Adventure* brand, and was made more interesting and more complex through game elements of chance in series like *Fighting Fantasy* and *Lone Wolf*.[49] These latter examples introduced randomness into the stories through rolling dice, and a generation of young people —particularly boys like me—grew up with dice rolling as an integral part of their reading experience. The popularity of the books faded away in the 1990s as computer games improved, replacing the written word with interactive, highly visual adventures, and replacing the randomness of dice rolls with hidden random number generators to make the experience as seamless as possible.

In more recent years, those young people have grown up, and have emerged as an online community with an appetite to rekindle their misspent youth.[50] One way to do that has been

---

[49] Not precisely "new", in fact. The concept of interactive fiction had existed for an extremely long time before even *Choose Your Own Adventure* came along, but it certainly wouldn't have been considered mainstream before.

[50] For those interested in picking up an interactive fiction book, I heartily recommend one of the most exciting recent authors, Samuel Isaacson.

through creating digital versions of these interactive books, such as Cubus Games' *Steam Highwayman*.[51] The challenge is that how to do this is not clear—some users don't like these digital versions to be too much like those richly animated computer games with hidden game mechanics, while others don't want to watch virtual dice being rolled and have to manually keep track of numbered references. Neither is "better" *per se*, the point is that forcing a user to submit to a digital experience that they don't like won't help them.

If we're familiar with a physical constellations product, we might want to use a digital version of it because it reminds us of our training from ten years ago. For some coachees that will be perfect, while for others the lack of a "digital first" mindset might frustrate them. This brings us back to what we were saying when comparing digital whiteboards. When introducing technologies to a particular coaching session, or to a particular coachee, we need to think more broadly than simply whether or not it ticks a series of functional boxes. Coachees need to be able to benefit from using the tool, and each coachee will respond differently. For one, the simple act of placing shapes on the screen will be enough, while another will want to explore with every option available to them.

---

[51] https://www.cubusgames.com/steam-highwayman

Alternatives

Let's Constellate

Let's Constellate[52] is essentially a stripped-down digital whiteboard, with the ability to add different coloured shapes from a pre-populated tray, resize and rotate them, and add arrows to communicate connections.

It's currently available for free in beta form, meaning the developers still don't consider it a fully fledged product. For this reason, it's certainly limited in its functionality, and may encounter more issues than one would like, although this hasn't happened to me in my testing.

It does what it's designed to do quite effectively, so those coaches that are purely looking for a digital constellations option that does that one thing well should look no further.

Slide decks

Once again we find ourselves reminded of that most flexible of coachtech tools: slide decks. We could also include digital whiteboards in this thought, and we already considered it within chapters 3 and 4.

There are plenty of ways to implement constellations digitally that don't require a specialist

---

[52] https://www.constell.online/

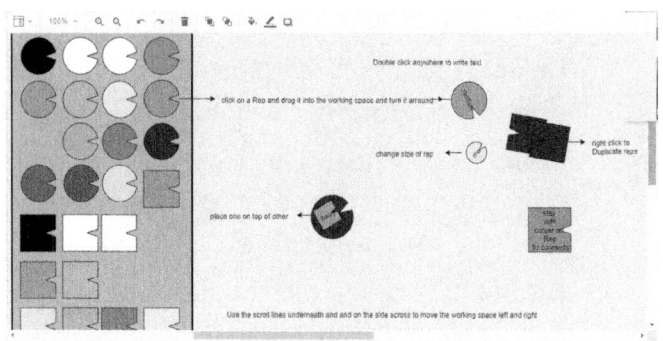

Figure 9.1 The Let's Constellate interface

tool. Conveniently, several people have already put a lot of thought into this and have kindly made their templates available for free. The shortest journey into this world for those who aren't in it yet would probably therefore be to use one of these. There will be no learning journey around the technology itself as we already know how to use it.

Online Fields,[53] for example, has produced a structured process accompanied by a pack of twelve slides to guide us through a small selection of exercises. To accompany this, or any digital constellations offering, we might also want to consider advice from The Whole Partnership[54] around how they recommend using this approach. They present the following five step CLEAR method:

- **Clarify**: getting clear about the question to be answered, the context and what a good

[53]https://onlinefields.net/

[54]https://www.wholepartnership.com/online-group-systemic-constellations-integrating-a-shared-image/

outcome would look like

- **Layout**: setting up the constellation visually, slowly introducing one element at a time
- **Explore**: asking questions about the elements in the constellation and their relationship to one another
- **Attune**: facilitating the coachee in becoming fully aware of the constellation
- **Resolve**: facilitating the coachee in inserting themselves into the constellation and deciding on actions to take

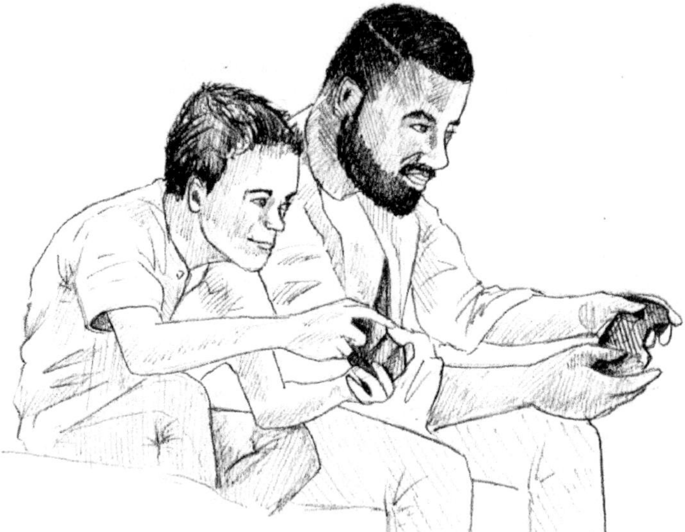

10

3D ENVIRONMENTS

Every so often, a piece of technology will raise its head to demonstrate clearly the enhanced power it can offer, and ProReal[55] is one of them. ProReal is a tool built on a computer games engine that allows a user to recreate their internal understanding of a situation, story, or system in three dimensions, through the introduction of animated people (called avatars in the tool) and objects to a virtual environment. Some self-reflection exercises are available for free on their website,[56] while annual licences and certification programmes are available at a price.

The selection of objects is limited to only a couple of dozen, but each has been carefully thought through, and the avatars can be heavily

[55] https://proreal.world/

[56] https://proreal.world/try/

customised. When they're first added to the landscape the user makes sure they fully represent the persona they're taking on, through editing:

- their name
- their colour
- their size
- a word or phrase to capture what they're saying or thinking
- an animated stance
- a mood-based emoji
- "inner voices" to float around their head giving skewed perspectives and pieces of advice

The tool can be used to create constellations like those described in the previous chapter, but it's intended to be more than that. It offers two landscapes to build in, one of which is a large, blank arena, and the other of which is designed for storytelling. In this second landscape, a selection of common turns of phrase have been visualised. There's a crossroads, and a fork in the road. A small forest below an imposing castle contains a clearing, within which the only flowers grow at the base of a beautiful shaft of sunlight. Drystone walls form small areas of grass, and break at the point where a stream flows, widening under a half-formed bridge until it cascades down a long waterfall in the shadow of an isolated tower.

In the storytelling landscape, a coach and coachee

can do far more than simply construct a systemic constellation. Exercises such as timelines and digital equivalents of chairwork and psychodrama can be played out through objects placed around the landscape, and its nature as a three-dimensional virtual space allows for exploration in much more immersive ways than simply visualising, or looking at nondescript shapes on a screen.

I was once coaching someone in the storytelling landscape and asked them to create their ideal future state. They put themselves and their family, all coloured yellow, relaxing in the shade of a tree. I then asked them to add their present selves to the landscape, and they opted for a dark orange, frustrated version of themselves, located in the middle of the stream. By moving the virtual camera from their present selves to their future selves and back again, the coachee was able to see things from quite literally a different perspective.

The harshest learning curve in this book?

This extraordinary power comes at an unfortunate cost. As ProReal has been designed to maximise the possibilities of the technology, it requires more user skill and experience than any other tool we've looked at within these pages. This doesn't make for a positive experience when trying to work with a coachee who hasn't used it before, and who is exploring a sensitive issue.

The truth with using a tool like this is that it's unlike some other technologies we've talked about. Most technologies from the previous chapters add a new or different angle to a coaching conversation, powered by technology. This chapter essentially asks a coachee to be fully present in their coaching session *and* to play a computer game at the same time. For some coachees—and for some coaches—that will be a step too far.

For example, we might be working with a coachee producing a constellation in Let's Constellate, a tool in the last chapter. As they're dragging shapes from the drawer, they might accidentally release the mouse button a mite too early. The result of this will be a stray shape in plain sight, and so the coachee without too much difficulty will pick it up again and move it to its intended destination. In ProReal, the three dimensional nature of the space might cause the same object released too early to shoot off into the distance, lost forever. In truth, the object doesn't have to be lost forever. An experienced user would rapidly locate the object and bring it back into view, but it's prudent to assume that the average coachee will not fall into this category.

This characteristic—not just of ProReal, but of any more complex tool—can make it a less-than-helpful addition to the average coaching session. Unlike something like a slide deck, which is extremely accessible given people's day-to-day experience of it, these tools cannot be launched at a moment's notice. When I received some coaching several years ago (in person), the coach took some photos of me at various points in the conversation and asked me to reflect on what my body was communicating. It was enlightening. A similar thing could be done through screenshots swiftly dropped into a slide deck and shared live in a coaching session. The coachee has seen this sort of technology several times before, and so there is no technology hurdle to have to leap over. But ProReal is different. It's an entirely new interface, with its own language, keyboard shortcuts, possibilities and nuances.

The rewards of something like ProReal can be transformative for a coachee. The effect of changing perspective, discovering that what one stakeholder can see is dramatically different from another, is difficult to overstate. But if using the tool is going to pull the rug out from a coachee's feet, upsetting them by making them feel out of their depth, we ought to be cautious about seeing it as a silver bullet.

Slowing down to speed up

The training material recommends that coachees watch a ten minute explanatory video before they use it for the first time, then take part in a fifteen minute exercise to get them used to the technology before they do anything for real. For many coachees, this is prohibitively long. Taking the time out for coaching is already a privilege, and essentially the time of an extra coaching session solely in order to use a particular piece of technology on this one occasion will not feel justified.

That time taken to get people up and running is important, if one is to use this sort of technology. Bypassing a robust onboarding process might feel like the right thing to do in order to accelerate the benefits of the tool, but let me tell you from hard-won personal experience that it's more trouble than it's worth, particularly if working with a group or a team. Under the right circumstances, ProReal is a delightful enabler for transformative conversations, and a single person using the tool who is less than proficient is unfortunately likely to derail the experience for all involved.

One particular feature that will quickly disrupt things is the shared perspective, where all users' views are the same. In this case, when an individual moves the camera, the viewpoint for everybody moves without warning. If another user's partway through moving an object at that moment, it could end up anywhere.

The keys to using ProReal effectively are therefore:

- Contract clearly at the outset what good behaviour looks like when using the tool (for example: hands on your laps unless explicitly asked to do something).

- Remain playful at all times![57] For this reason, this sort of tool should be avoided if dealing with something particularly sensitive, unless you're absolutely sure of the coachee's capabilities.

Most coaches that use ProReal won't use it as a one-off activity. To get the most out of something like ProReal, it will often be worth revisiting it session after session, increasing the likelihood of coachee insights commensurate with their steadily increasing capabilities.

Unless they're a gamer

The exception to everything we've just said would be if we're working with a coachee who plays a lot of computer games in their spare time. The keyboard shortcuts, while unfamiliar to the day-to-day work environment, will be second nature to someone who's played computer games every day since they were a teenager. In these instances, almost the exact opposite approach is needed. Rather than a long, drawn-out onboarding process, the coachee should be encouraged to immediately begin to experiment.Slowing things down will lose their interest and break rapport, so should be used

---

[57]For a more detailed description of the importance of playfulness in coachtech, see https://www.linkedin.com/pulse/importance-playfulness-coachtech-sam-isaacson/

sparingly, as a technique to disrupt their getting sidetracked.

This presents a new problem, however. While the technology will flummox a coachee for whom it's new, if the coachee quickly begins to discover new functionality we were previously unaware of, there's a chance things will begin to move too quickly for us, putting us in the place of feeling discombobulated instead! With this in mind, let's move onto the one rule that needs to rise above all others.

Rapport is everything

New technologies can feel chaotic, limiting, and disruptive in unhelpful ways. These characteristics should never be occurring in a coaching session. A level of unpredictability can be positive, when managed well—often, the best learning happens at the cusp of not knowing—but this practice of managing the experience well becomes extremely important when a layer of technology sits between us and our coachees.

Acknowledging this, a general rule would be to not introduce something like this to a coachee for the first time without thinking through the logistics in advance. Setting it up in advance of the coaching session is an absolute must, as is getting comfortable enough with the tool ourselves so that we can act as technical support if—*when*—issues occur. And when they do, nothing's going to make it worse than us "helping" by taking all the control away from them. We're meant to be there to empower our coachees, not to confirm their limiting assumptions about their lack of ability. Instead, let's commit to pausing patiently, gently offering support if they need it, and injecting encouragement and humour throughout to settle them.

If it turns out that our coachees are more skilled and experienced with using a particular technology, our responsibility changes to having to increase our own expertise. It's never good to have an unhealthy power dynamic in a coaching relationship, but when it comes to adding technology we run a real risk of sabotaging the session if we're not capable of dealing with technical issues when they arise, even when they're caused by our coachee's superior knowledge and ambition with it.

Alternatives

SystemicVR

SystemicVR[58] is, strictly speaking, a 3D constellations tool, but can be used at least as widely as ProReal can. In its design it can do a very similar suite of actions, but it's been developed expecting the user to create a traditional constellation within a virtual room. The selection of

[58] https://www.systemicvr.net/

Figure 10.1 A screenshot from an indoor scene in SystemicVR

Figure 10.2 A screenshot from an outdoor scene in SystemicVR

environments is greater than the binary choice offered by ProReal, although the environments themselves are smaller. A collection of videos are available to preview the tool on their YouTube channel,[59] a free trial is available from their website, and pricing is offered on a per hour or unlimited use basis.

[59] https://www.youtube.com/channel/
UCoEwh3oRi3HPp_glbRh4Mrw

Figure 10.3 A screenshot from Fortnite

MMORPGs

A cheaper option with potentially fewer technical hurdles to overcome would be to make the most of the enormous number of massively multiplayer online roleplaying games (or MMORPGs) out there. These games offer vast, virtual spaces that players can explore, with some game elements such as points scoring for solving puzzles or defeating enemies, and the opportunity to interact in various ways with other players of the game, joining from around the world. Perhaps the best known of these outside of the gaming community would be Second Life,[60] within which coaching conversations have been trialled. Another option with plenty of opportunities for creativity would be Minecraft.[61]

The advantages with this route are that their

[60] https://secondlife.com/

[61] https://www.minecraft.net/

development budgets are vastly greater than those available to the teams for something like ProReal, meaning their technical capabilities and user experience are likely to be much more mature. They're also more likely to be more affordable and, in some cases, more accessible. A gamer is quite likely to already have access to Minecraft—it's a very popular game—while even the geekiest of gaming nerds is unlikely to have a ProReal licence.

Playful use of these games might produce exciting, creative coaching experiences. They wouldn't be appropriate for everyone, but incorporating some of those game elements into a coaching session could add a dash of something unique. A game like Fortnite,[62] for example, allows for a private conversation to take place between 2-4 people while competing against others as a team. A skilled coach using the Fortnite island—or even a custom-built environment made using its Creative mode—as a metaphor for the coachee's issue could facilitate a very different sort of coaching conversation, with moments influenced by events happening in the game.

---

[62]https://www.epicgames.com/fortnite/

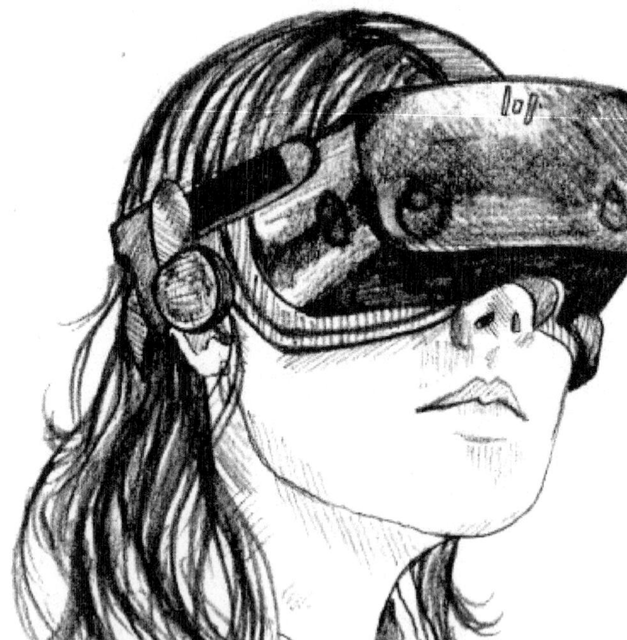

11

EXERCISES IN VIRTUAL REALITY

Technology trends are increasingly pointing towards the unhelpfully undefined word: Metaverse. Facebook rebranded to Meta to clearly communicate where their intended strategy lies, investment is being poured into a whole range of metaverse technologies, and VR devices are being released by every big name in technology.

This shift, along with many others, will undoubtedly impact the way coaching is delivered, in much the same way as the lockdowns of 2020 did to rapidly accelerate take-up of video coaching and digital coaching providers. Even before we see a majority changing their behaviours, coaches have an opportunity to make use of virtual reality technologies to enhance our coaching.

Prior to remote coaching taking over as the dominant mode of delivery, coaches often used to travel around with a box of tricks. A wad of sticky notes and premium pens, a deck of picture cards and a bag of beads and buttons, and it felt like we were ready to leave the house. Adding a virtual reality headset to that setup might mean needing to leave the pens behind, but as we'll go on to see we might not even need them anyway.

In this chapter, we'll look at a handful of different virtual reality apps we could experiment with, before addressing the biggest investment of all: the headset itself.

BodySwaps

One of the key competencies of the best leaders—in fact, of the best humans full stop—is emotional intelligence, in all its forms.[63] One element of this is empathy. The ability in particular to see oneself from the perspectives of others drastically increases leadership effectiveness.

BodySwaps[64] is a virtual reality app that aims to provide this insight in a particularly tangible way. When we initiate one of the situational experiences, the user takes on the point of view of a person about to take part in a conversation. After observing an opening sequence happening around them, the user selects their response from a selection of options,

[63] Takšic, V. (2002). *The Importance of Emotional Intelligence (Competence) in Positive Psychology.*

[64] https://bodyswaps.co/

and then continues interacting with whatever happens next in whichever way comes most naturally. The voice and gesticulations are recorded in the tool, and then comes the clever part. The perspective of the user shifts to that of the person they're interacting with, and they then relive the conversation, this time experiencing what it's like to be on the receiving end of their natural response.

This is the next evolution of watching a video recording of ourselves back. It retains a bit of that unavoidable cringe factor—it's rare to find someone who doesn't claim to dislike recordings of themselves—but the avatar provides a more natural ability to reflect more objectively.

An onboarding process is built into the tool, which takes quite some time and cannot be skipped. The tool has clearly been designed as a standalone experience, rather than a microlearning to sit within a coaching session lasting less than an hour. As an end-to-end experience it's unarguably well managed, but as a result it takes up a lot more time than I'd think most coaches would be willing to give up for it with the exception of a one-off session focused on this topic.

VirtualSpeech

It's frequently claimed that public speaking is one of the most common fears, and it's certainly something a lot of people tend to avoid. It's clear, however, that the ability to perform in front of an audience is a valuable one to develop, particularly for leaders. VirtualSpeech[65] aims to provide coachees with an experience of public speaking that's as realistic as possible without being the real thing.

Leadership development professionals tend to encourage people to rehearse speeches and presentations before they're delivered, perhaps in front of a mirror. For those who are particularly invested, recording oneself in front of a camera and reflecting on the video afterwards is recommended. But anyone who has delivered a mock presentation in this way will testify that the experience is not comparable. The energy of a room full of people - or, perhaps worse, a room full of empty chairs with only a couple of people dotted around - is significantly different from the privacy of one's bedroom. Time seems to behave differently, and the adrenalin of the moment leads to unexpected physiological effects that are difficult to predict.

VirtualSpeech offers a selection of immersive environments to give the user experiences of delivering presentations in front of crowds of hundreds in a large hall, half a dozen in a meeting room, in front of an interview panel, and even in a press conference. The tool places the user in a 360° image of a location that's populated by animated photographs of people, looking expectantly at them as they would if expecting a speech to be delivered. Slide decks can be uploaded to prepare for specific

[65] https://virtualspeech.com/

EXERCISES IN VIRTUAL REALITY 151

Figure 11.1 The view in VirtualSpeech while delivering a presentation

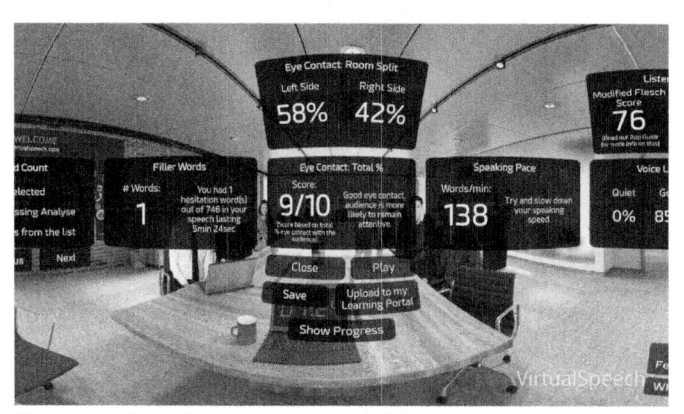

Figure 11.2 Speech analysis built into VirtualSpeech

presentations, and visible timers can be set to support the delivery. There are helpful analytics built into it that are designed to raise awareness around making eye contact with the audience, speaking at the right pace, and avoiding filler words. It's also possible as a user to watch oneself back in the form of an avatar, to aid in self-reflection.

Using this with a coachee will demand a short

amount of time to onboard them, before either sitting patiently in the room with them while they deliver at least a portion of their presentation, or connecting with them remotely through the VirtualSpeech live training feature. Once it's finished, we can then use a classic coaching conversation to explore what happened, informed by the analytics.

D&I: Perspectives

D&I: Perspectives[66] is a collection of interactive experiences seen through the eyes of various people experiencing microaggressions, accompanied by some explanation and reflective questions designed to elevate the user's understanding and empathy related to diversity and inclusion (D&I). The presentation is a computer generated office environment, overlaid by real-world actors filmed in 3D.

It doesn't have the same sort of interactivity and analysis offered by BodySwaps or VirtualSpeech, instead acting as an educational immersive experience to trigger a relevant coaching conversation. A designed experience like D&I: Perspectives or even 360° videos watched with a VR headset prove to be a much more effective way to increase understanding around an issue than simply being taught it in a classroom, reading it in a book or

[66] https://makereal.co.uk/work/d-and-i-perspectives/

watching a two-dimensional video. In several studies, VR experiences such as one showing the effects of climate change on coral reefs have been shown to increase the likelihood that participants would donate to charity.[67] For a coach being brought in to deliver coaching on inclusive leadership, a tool like D&I: Perspectives might be the sprinkling of fairy dust required to catalyse the sort of change they're looking to see.

The app doesn't cost very much, so someone with a headset can get it now, and there are options for businesses looking to roll it out to a larger population.

Virtual reality for mindfulness

Thinking along different lines, VR can be used to support a coaching session through leading immersive exercises designed to bring the user into the present moment. Rather than having to ask a coachee to close their eyes and ignore the sights and sounds of the room, particularly if they're working from home and have been surrounded by the same four walls for every meeting, donning the headset can be a great help. The distractions of the day become irrelevant, and VR introduces that important element of playfulness, catalysing calm

[67]Nelson, K. M., Anggraini, E., & Schlüter, A. (2020). Virtual reality as a tool for environmental conservation and fundraising. *PLOS ONE*, 15(4)

and a positive attitude towards experimentation.

One example of this sort of tool would be Tripp,[68] a guided meditation experience in which the visual field and accompanying soundscape is designed to invoke a sense of calm. This is accompanied by a calming voice encouraging conscious breathing and increased awareness. A potentially more advanced option would be DEEP,[69] which uses breathing as an integral data input of the experience. While many people know that good breathing techniques are important, understanding what difference it can make can be difficult. In DEEP, the user is offered the chance to explore fantastical spaces purely through their breathing, providing direct feedback and inspiring greater awareness.

These are only a couple of examples—a quick browse through a virtual reality app store like the Oculus Store[70] or VIVEPORT[71] will reveal plenty more.

Virtual reality for creativity

A final collection of VR tools that are worth mentioning would be those designed for creativity. As we've seen in earlier chapters, these approaches

[68]https://www.tripp.com/

[69]https://www.exploredeep.com/

[70]https://www.oculus.com/experiences/quest/

[71]https://www.viveport.com/

unlock alternative approaches to thinking, and the immersive approach of VR offers a freedom that might not be possible using other means.

Probably the most widely talked about example of this would be Tilt Brush,[72] a 3D painting tool from Google, in which the user can walk around the object they've created using simple paint-like tools, along with more unpredictable options. This embodied experience of creativity and exploration offers true opportunities for insights.

Another example would be Cosmic Sugar,[73] which simply allows the user to manipulate millions of particles as if controlling gravity in a vacuum. We've seen the meaning-making tendency of humans earlier in this book, so it will come as no surprise that a coachee could interpret something entirely abstract yet somehow controllable like this in all manner of different ways. Perhaps Cosmic Sugar would be best introduced when encountering situations the coachee is finding hard to express otherwise.

A final example—of course, there are many more—would be Fujii.[74] In Fujii, the user takes on the role of a virtual gardener, exploring a selection of virtual gardens and nurturing new seeds accompanied by fictional plant and insect life to encourage

---

[72] https://www.tiltbrush.com/

[73] https://cosmicsugarvr.com/

[74] https://funktroniclabs.com/presskit/sheet.php?p=fujii

mindfulness and perhaps providing access to new metaphors.

How to select a headset

Selecting a headset is a bit like selecting a smartphone. In some senses, any one will do. And then it turns out there are compatibility issues across each platform, limited lifespans, and an enormous, unwanted variety in the quality on offer.

Let's start with the bottom of the range, a product originally pioneered by Google called Cardboard. The name is decidedly unoriginal, coming from the fact that a piece of cardboard wrapped around almost any smartphone and a pair of lenses give birth to a VR headset. The clear advantage behind a headset made from cardboard is that the price is extremely affordable. My first VR coaching took place using Cardboard, and the affordability enabled a much larger group to experience it than would have been possible otherwise—one of my volunteers was in her 80s, not the target demographic for any VR headset producer I'm aware of!

There are now a range of plastic alternatives at more premium price points, but the underlying principles are the same. The image quality and VR movement are limited by the smartphone, and none of the best quality VR apps are available for Cardboard. One exception to this would be vTime

XR, which we'll come back to in the next chapter. If you've never experienced VR and would like to, Cardboard is an affordable way to dip one's toe in.

Full-on VR headsets vary in price, and the most popular consumer headset at the moment would be the Meta Quest 2, which costs about the same as a midrange smartphone and is extremely impressive. The fact it comes from Meta, which owns Facebook, will be off-putting for some due to its reputation and history with regard to data privacy. As with all technology, personal preference will come into play here. Meta is investing heavily in the metaverse, so it should remain functional and supported for at least as long as any other product.

Two other brands to keep an eye on will be Apple and Microsoft. Apple have been working on a VR headset for a while and have announced, like Meta, they will launch an untethered headset in 2024, which will undoubtedly drive consumer behaviour. Mp3 players, smartphones, smartwatches and Bluetooth headphones all existed before Apple's market entries, and suddenly those products became mainstream as soon as Apple moved. Microsoft, on the other hand, have already released headsets but are expanding their metaverse presence through experimenting on the outskirts of Microsoft Teams. The corporate footprint they hold shouldn't be underestimated as a route people will end up going down, and I wouldn't want to bet that "Teams VR" will be guaranteed to work well on a headset made by Meta, Apple, Google, Samsung,

Xiaomi, or any of the other big providers.

The uncomfortable thing with any of these companies is that they operate a "Web 2.0" mentality, meaning users can only interact by going through a centralised organisation. The growth of the metaverse is happening side-by-side with blockchain-powered Web 3.0 philosophies, which could allow users to interact directly through decentralised autonomous organisations (or DAOs, to those in the know). A decentralised approach to the metaverse doesn't mean it will exclusively work outside of Web 2.0 structures, and it's unlikely to topple existing dominance hierarchies immediately, but for those wanting to engage in this particular aspect of technology it's an arena worth following.

12

VIRTUAL REALITY FOR MEETINGS

The previous chapter outlined a handful of ways we can make use of some of the most cutting edge of emergent technology to add something truly different to our coaching. A sprinkling of VR will make a coaching session stand out through a pleasant and innovative experience, and that's probably good. Coaching is essentially a learning process, and innovative experiences are more likely to be remembered.[75] But VR and the metaverse more broadly are much more than that.

With both Meta and Apple promising standalone smart glasses within two years and tethered smart

---

[75]Brown R., Kulik J. 1977. Flashbulb memories. *Cognition.* 1977;5:73-99

glasses available now, there's a reasonable chance that before too long we will need to rethink our entire approach to remote coaching. VR as a whimsical, added value activity to an otherwise non-VR experience won't work when people end up spending ten hours per day wearing a headset.

The direction of travel is currently towards metaverse technology being used for all manner of things, foremost of which for coaching purposes would be communications. Bill Gates casually predicted that by the end of 2024 most live remote conversations will take place via digital avatars,[76] and if that seems like too much of a shift just think about how much video conferencing has moved on in the last few years.

Ten years ago most people knew that video conferencing was possible, but it wasn't commonplace. Conducting a video call tended to mean booking out the special room, along with trained technical support. This bleeding edge of communications technology was reserved for an elite few who felt the urge to use the latest technology, and had the budget to make it an option.

The circumstances of 2020 accelerated the adoption of video conferencing, but it only served to move the timeline forward. Video was coming whether people liked it or not, and whether people

---

[76] https://www.gatesnotes.com/About-Bill-Gates/Year-in-Review-2021#ALChapter5

admitted it or not.

The current state of VR feels surprisingly familiar to the place that video was a decade ago. It requires specialist hardware, which comes with a price tag, and benefits from a techie mind to begin to use it. But with the extremely public rebrand of Facebook's holding company to Meta, massive investment from almost all the big tech companies, and now hints of mainstream devices within a couple of years, it feels like the writing's on the wall. VR—or, more likely, AR (augmented reality, where digital images are overlaid on the real world)—will be readily accessible for a larger proportion of the population, and consumer habits will shift as a result.

As people's preferences around communications technology change, our modes of coaching will necessarily have to respond as a result.[77] At the time of writing this, I'm aware of barely a dozen coaches in the world that have truly used metaverse technology to deliver professional coaching, but this is only a matter of time. A coach wanting to experience the next generation of technology should look no further than VR for the moment. Even the most sceptical among us should at least think about how they might want to be prepared, so that when that first metaverse coaching session appears in the diary we all feel like we know how we're going to approach it.

---

[77] Isaacson, S. 2021. *How to Thrive as a Coach in a Digital World: Coaching with Technology.* Open University Press

vTime XR

We'll start with vTime XR[78] because it's possibly the most accessible of all the options we'll look at. The app itself is free, and as we pointed out in the last chapter, it can be experienced in all its immersive glory through not much more than a smartphone and a piece of cardboard. Order a kit for not much more than a nice coffee, and we have a rudimentary VR headset!

In vTime XR, we step into the body of an avatar that sits in a stationary position in a range of environments. Some are intentionally designed for the platform, with animated features and sounds, and it's possible to upload 360° photographs as well. It's nice to sit in a meditative Japanese garden and hear the trickling stream dancing along, and it's also powerful to travel to a specific location that means a lot to a coachee's particular situation, and carry out the coaching there. My favourite locations selected by coachees have been floating above New York City, sitting in the midst of Diagon Alley, and, of course, coaching in orbit.

That's pretty much where the features of the platform begin and end, and as we've seen with some other products that's part of its beauty. It's possible to share a slide or two in some of the settings, but this is a platform designed with only one purpose in mind: Have a conversation in groups of two to four people.

[78] https://vtime.net/

The advantages of this are twofold. Firstly, it's a perfect entry route for coaching. All we really need is a space for a conversation with a coachee, and it does that very effectively. Secondly, it feels as inclusive as it will ever do. Yes, a premium headset will allow a user to move the avatar's hands themselves rather than rely on the automatic gesticulation, but this isn't a deal-breaker for me. A user accessing the free platform from a cheap, cardboard headset will have pretty much as good an experience as someone else who's paid a small fortune for the privilege of better graphics.

MeetinVR

A more advanced approach to the idea of private meeting spaces in VR would be MeetinVR,[79] a solution that allows access from a selection of headsets and also a PC desktop option. The feel of the tool is clean and professional. While some of the other platforms carry with them an element of whimsy, which might make them seem like a gimmick in some contexts, MeetinVR doesn't suffer from that for the most part.

It offers a range of meeting locations such as rooms with chairs around tables of various sizes, a large workshop-style area with whiteboards and space to gather in small groups, a lecture theatre, a more informal space that feels like a rooftop bar, and

[79] https://www.meetinvr.com/

more. You can also select the wider environment within which the space is located, giving you views over well-known cities, rural areas, above the clouds and even in orbit. There's even the option to abandon the room environment altogether through the use of an uploaded 360° photo.

Some of the features significantly close the gap between what's possible in person versus what's possible in video conferencing platforms. For example, it's straightforward to add notecards that can be physically moved around the space, replicating to a certain extent the tactile experience of the picture cards from chapter 5. There's a pen that can be used to draw on whiteboards and even in mid-air, and images can be dropped into the space that can be reshaped, stuck to walls and moved around the space as part of, for example, a constellations exercise. One particularly clever feature allows the facilitator to create smaller "voice zones", meaning a group can enter private breakout rooms or take a personal call without disturbing the rest of the group or removing their headset, and while retaining a view of the others in the space.

It's possible to access the platform for free as a guest to create and join meetings, but if you want to schedule meetings in advance and customise spaces, you'll need to buy a licence.

Spatial

A solution intending a fuller experience of remote ways to meet and with more collaboration options is Spatial.[80] Its vision for meeting spaces is a mite grander than that of vTime XR or MeetinVR, offering spaces like art galleries, parks and office buildings as locations. The moment you create an account (for free) you're asked to take a selfie and create a lifelike avatar, and the Spatial website uses the word "metaverse" a lot more than the others on this list, communicating their intent to be a digital life experience, more than purely a remote meeting technology.

Spatial is designed more for teams than for one-to-ones, but it's certainly effective with smaller numbers. Even with a free account, you can create your own spaces and events, inviting up to 50 others to join you at one time. You can add in images, video, and other files to shared spaces, introduce sticky notes, and explore the geography of a space.

The graphics look like they're designed to be more detailed and realistic than vTime XR or MeetinVR, which will appeal to some people, although it risks for some users tipping into the "uncanny valley", the dip in pleasure we experience when something looks like it ought to be lifelike and yet isn't. It's also the most powerful and far-reaching of the tools in this chapter, with features allowing fully customised environments and even sales of

[80]https://spatial.io/

NFTs[81] live in the tool. As we saw in our discussion earlier, these expanded features may prove a blocker for less confident users.

AltspaceVR

A more playful yet no less powerful tool would be Microsoft's AltspaceVR,[82] a virtual universe full of events and other gatherings across a range of worlds with several unique features. The experience feels a lot more cartoony, and intentionally so. There are interactive games to play on the platform and expansive spaces to explore, which might be perfect for a virtual walking coaching session!

With the power of Microsoft behind it and its potential future connection through Mesh[83] to Teams, this feels to me like a platform worth getting comfortable with, as there's a good chance a critical mass will end up either there or in Meta's equivalent alternative, Horizon Worlds.[84]

---

[81]NFTs (Non Fungible Tokens) are uniquely traceable digital assets powered by decentralised blockchain technology. Their trustworthiness as proof of ownership makes it likely that they will be used much more widely in the future, although at the present time they are almost exclusively used only for collectors of digital artwork.

[82]https://altvr.com/

[83]https://www.microsoft.com/en-us/mesh

[84]https://www.oculus.com/horizon-worlds/

The differences between these products are ultimately quite subtle. The fundamental experience of each is an enjoyable, natural, embodied conversation while wearing a headset, so the ability to play chess or draw a picture in each will generally be trumped by a more pragmatic approach to which is most convenient and accessible. As a result, the conclusion we should draw with any of these products ought to be to simply get comfortable with using VR technology now, to prepare us for the inevitable. We don't want our first experience of meeting in the metaverse to be a high-pressure coaching session.

A digital migration to the metaverse will happen in the coming years. We would do well to start our practice now, so we're ready for that shift in consumer and organisational behaviour when it comes.

Section 3

Setting off

13

THE ETHICS OF COACHTECH

In this book, we've looked at a broad range of technologies. Some will have felt more exciting, more natural, and more appropriate for you than others will have, and that's truly great. Every coach is different. More than that, every coachee is different, and every coach-coachee relationship is uniquely beautiful in a way that means we can't for a moment believe that adding a particular piece of technology is always going to be a good idea. Even when it is a good idea, *how* we introduce it and use it will also have to be thought through.

With that in mind, it's important to think about coaching with technology at a principles level. There are more technologies available now—with more emerging all the time—than would be possible to capture in a book like this. Taking things to a more abstract level will be helpful as we continue to apply what we're learning to our coaching practice.

Purpose-led

Any time the thought of using technology crosses our minds, we should train ourselves to ask the question: Why am I wanting to do this? A lot of ethics in practice comes down to the intentions that lie behind our actions. Both are important, because the actions are the things that cause an impact regardless of the intentions behind them, but I'd rather have good intentions than bad any day of the week.

I know, we're coaches, we do everything with positive intent. Now we've said that, let's think about reality. The world of coaches contains a glorious, richly diverse collection of individuals wanting to sacrificially help people, organisations and the more than human world. It also unfortunately contains an unignorable undercurrent of selfish personal gain, surfaced through the vast array of what I'll generously call coach training programmes out there that promise seven figure salaries, the opportunity to share the stage with international bestselling authors and speakers, and of course a sense of deep, personal fulfilment. I'll be the first to admit that while I'd prefer to place myself in the former category, the latter is frustratingly tempting, and I expect I'm not alone in that.

Let's watch ourselves. When a coachee mentions a tricky situation and our minds conjure up WOMBO Dream as a way to represent that reality in all its inexplicable complexity, is that genuinely because we believe it's going to unlock insight for this person at this moment? Or is there something else going on?

Do we want to use it to silence the negative narrative we have playing through our minds that says we can't support them without the crutch of a piece of showy technology?

Might it actually be that we just enjoy playing with the tool?

Worse, are we being driven by a desire to demonstrate our superior skill and knowledge?

Good times to add technology into coaching conversations are those moments where the coaching questions themselves are taking a coachee round and round in circles, and where even the voice in our heads that always knows what the coachee should be doing is staying quiet. The creativity unleashed through experimentation and slight discomfort might be just what's needed. And the vulnerability of admitting that our desire to use a particular piece of technology is down to our own sense of getting stuck might be just what's needed to increase the trust to a level that allows for the coaching conversation to get a place it previously hadn't.

The golden rule of coachtech

In addition to all of that, there are some situations where technology is as close to an absolute necessity or an absolute never. We've said this already in this book but it bears repeating: When rapport is on the line, always favour it. The rapport between coach and coachee is one of the biggest factors in coaching outcomes,[85] and technology can form a big part of that.

We've probably all experienced tech nerds whizzing through a new piece of technology far too quickly for us, making us feel uncomfortable and out of our depth. Equally, we've probably all experienced people stuck in the mindset of decades-old technology taking far too long and making unbelievable mistakes when using technology we're familiar with, making us feel bored and somewhere between angry and empathetic about their frustrating lack of understanding. Neither of those extremes should be present in a coaching session, where coach and coachee should maintain an adult-adult relationship throughout.

This means in practice that we should be putting in as much effort as possible to becoming really good with technology, in order to match the abilities of

---

[85] See Graßmann, C., Schölmerich, F., Schermuly, C. C. The relationship between working alliance and client outcomes in coaching: A meta-analysis. *Human Relations*. 2020;73(1):35-58, in which rapport forms a critical part of what they define as the "working alliance".

the most capable coachee, while remaining aware of their ability levels and taking things at a pace that matches them. This might mean selecting a video coaching technology that both coach and coachee are equally comfortable with, introducing new technologies when this ignites new energy in a coachee, and holding back from potentially more transformative technologies when recognising the negative impact it might have on a coaching conversation.

Valuing confidentiality

Few things in the world of coachtech get coaches more animated than a conversation around confidentiality. The moment any data, including live-streamed audio and video, is captured in a system or travels from one location to another, there's a risk it might be accessed by someone other than the coach or coachee, sometimes by design, and that's a different position from the in-person habits coaches have formed. Telling no-one any detail by default has been a foundation of coaching for a long time, so technology removing that makes coaches uneasy.

I was on hold on the phone for a medical facility recently. One of the recorded messages that played while I was waiting for someone to pick up the phone said: "We want you to know that everything you share with us will be kept confidential. Please be aware that we record all conversations for training and quality purposes." Those two sentences surely can't both be true! And yet technology tends to need access to data in order to be as helpful as possible.

There are some technologies highlighted in this book that don't need any personal data whatsoever, such as building a random poem. Others, like a digital whiteboard, have been built with saving and sharing in mind and so our awareness should be taking privacy into account.

Our focus in coaching ought to be on maximising the effectiveness of the relationship. If a coachee's going to get value out of using a piece of technology and they're comfortable sharing whatever data is needed to achieve that, who are we to stand in their way? But let's make sure we're responsible for preventing a voice assistant from secretly recording everything we're saying at the same time.

A co-creative approach

The coachtech landscape for most coaches should feel different for each coachee. I know there are some coaches who are selling themselves as "the such-and-such coach" to show that if a coachee wants to work with a specific piece of technology they're in the right place, but most of us tend to be a bit more eclectic than that.

Our role with most of our coachees will be to co-create a landscape with them that's going to work for the partnership we're creating, given their personality, priorities, focus areas, and technology ability and appetite. This is easier said than done, as we're naturally limited by our own lack of knowledge as well as the coachee's. If neither of us knows a technology exists, how can we use it?

The key here is to build a specific technology-infused approach for each coachee that they've been a part of at every stage. Yes, it's lovely to suggest halfway through a coaching session that a digital picture card deck might be a fun way to explore this topic, but doing that when magnetic poetry might be preferred by the coachee might be a missed opportunity.

Here's the conclusion then. Research a good selection of different technologies that we'd each like in our toolkits, don't hold back from offering our coachees technology given the guidelines above, and make sure the coachee has the final say on what gets introduced when. In my experience, most coachees are open-minded and enthusiastic about trying this stuff out, so it's important we give them the chance to benefit from it when appropriate.

14

DEFINING COACHTECH

What is coachtech?

We're in the final chapter of the book, which feels a bit too late to be answering that question, but there's a good reason we've waited until now to look at it. Despite how it may seem, it's about more than semantics.

Alright, maybe it's a bit about semantics.

The difference between coachtech and CoachTech

When is a door not a door? When it's ajar, as I remember Doctor Who revealing.[86] When is coachtech not CoachTech?

[86] https://tardis.fandom.com/wiki/The_Mind_Robber_(TV_story)

There are several technologies out there that would claim to be coaching technologies: coaching platforms, digital coaching conferences, AI coaches, and some of those we've looked at in this book. Maybe we could capitalise the C and T to describe these as CoachTech, to differentiate them from a lot of other technologies mentioned here.

Coachtech, in its broadest sense, could be any technology used by a coach for coaching purposes. That's the argument I used when pulling together the coachtech landscape in my previous book. The majority of the technology we visited in the previous section has fallen into that category. WOMBO Dream, Magnetic Poetry, and MyNoise existed before coaches started using them, and I'd be extremely surprised if any of them had professional coaching as a use case.

I pull out this difference—the difference between coachtech and CoachTech—because of the core reason why coaching works differently from any other development tool. Training is great. Line management is great. But coaching is extra special, because it's personalised and non-directive. Allow me therefore to welcome us into the irony of CoachTech.

CoachTech has been designed with such a singular focus that, in order to get best use out of it, we're always best to do things the way it wants us to. You might have seen this if you've used any of the self reflection apps out there. One I was testing out asked me first to rate my sense of calm on a

DEFINING COACHTECH 181

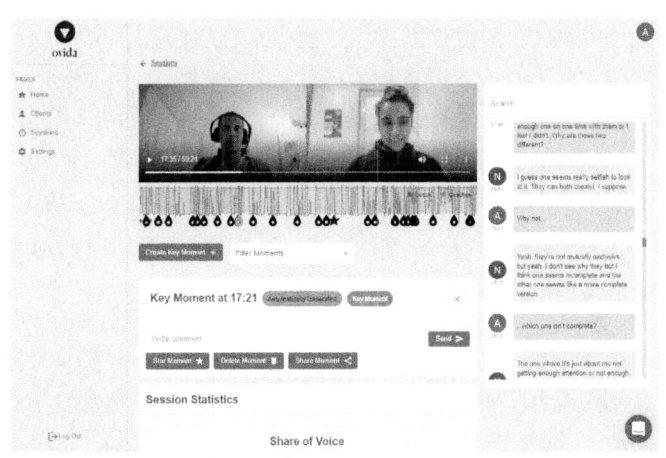

Figure 14.1 The Ovida interface

scale of 1-10, then asked me to state which area of my life I wanted to work on, then asked another specific question, and on and on. If a user opens the app with anything else on their mind, they're not going to get as much use out of it as they would if they'd just submit to the process.

The same could be said of most CoachTech products out there. Coaching management platforms require us to think about our coaching practice in the same way as the platform was designed. Digital coaching providers need to be able to guarantee a certain level of consistency and reporting quality to their customers. AI coaching robots need strict boundaries to manage the conversations they provide. Coaching analysis tools like Ovida[87], which automatically identifies key moments in a session using speech and facial

[87] https://www.ovida.org/

expressions for use in asynchronous supervision, need us to use them in the way they were designed, or they become more a hindrance than a help.

Compare those to Magnetic Poetry. When we press load, all we get is a random selection of words and a blank space. It's almost as if no-one's thought through every psychological ramification of it. Now we come to think of it, it's nothing more than a silly timewaster, isn't it?

Yes it is, and that's what makes it perfect. It's playful—we've said that's important—and more than that, it allows us to use it in whatever form we want to. If a coachee has an issue they're struggling to resolve, we can encourage them to explore that creatively in a poem. If a coachee can't think of anything to work through, we can encourage them to explore that creatively in a poem. In fact, if a coachee has finished the conversation and we just want to ask them for feedback, we can encourage them to explore that creatively in a poem.

This isn't at all a criticism of CoachTech—plenty of it is absolutely brilliant—it's simply raising our awareness to the fact that coachtech doesn't need to be CoachTech in order to be helpful. I'm about to encourage us again to do our own research, and that shouldn't begin with an internet search for "coaching technology". That might generate some solutions, but perhaps not the best ones depending on what we're trying to achieve.

How to be superhuman

A slip of the finger almost named this final section "How to become superhuman", and that would be wrong. If we're a coach, we're already superhuman in our own ways. We have characteristics that are unique to each one of us, and in that sense are uniquely brilliant. Even some of the simplest coaching techniques give us an ability to cut through conversation and thinking that makes people wonder how we're able to think so creatively, even as we deeply know that the creativity actually lies in the person we're asking the questions of.

In the words of the Co-Active Training Institute, people are "creative, resourceful, and whole",[88] and that includes you and me. The purpose of this book is to provide a handful of ideas to catalyse some new ways of thinking, provoke some experimentation, and tickle the curiosity many coaches feel around how best to use technology. Its purpose is *not* to suggest the best products available out there. Many of the pages in this book will be entirely useless to some readers, but one or two might change their coaching practice for the better, forever. Overall, I'd hope the book as a whole has at least offered a step or two towards a more informed and optimistic attitude towards technology in coaching.

Maybe eight of these ten technologies are going to become permanent additions to your toolkit, and maybe none of them will. Either way: Fantastic.

[88] https://coactive.com/about/new-language-of-leadership/

Taking what we've learned here together, let's get our routes to research open and get to work forming our own coachtech toolkits. Internet searches, publications from the professional bodies and elsewhere, conferences, exhibitions and trade shows, the list goes on. Let's get looking at what's available, and start to experiment.

You know yourself better than most people do, and you know your coachees too. Bearing that in mind and now armed with everything we've look at together, go forth into this new world! Explore the known and unknown places, equip yourself with a uniquely curated selection of technologies, and become the best version of you, for the sake of our collective future.

Onward.

ABOUT THE AUTHOR

Sam Isaacson is an enthusiastic coach, coach supervisor, and adviser on coachtech and organisational coaching. The first person in the world to offer coaching in virtual reality, he writes about his explorations at the edges of what's possible with technology to maximise the possibilities of coaching.

Having gained experience from three of the most well-known professional services firms, he's now Global Director of Consulting for CoachHub, one of the world's biggest digital coaching providers.

He plays active roles across the profession, including as Chair of the UK Government's Coaching Professional apprenticeship trailblazer group, members of working groups and advisory boards for the ICF and EMCC Global, and frequently sharing his insights at coaching events and conferences.

He has four young sons and also writes interactive fiction books, one of which has been an Amazon #1 bestseller.

He can be found most reliably at **https://www.linkedin.com/in/samisaacson**, where he writes about coachtech from time to time.

Printed in Great Britain
by Amazon